RUBBED UP THE WRONG WAY

RUBBED UP THE WRONG WAY

A Physiotherapist's Story

PROFESSOR GRACE DOREY MBE

The Book Guild Ltd

First published in Great Britain in 2020 by
The Book Guild Ltd
9 Priory Business Park
Wistow Road, Kibworth
Leicestershire, LE8 0RX
Freephone: 0800 999 2982
www.bookguild.co.uk
Email: info@bookguild.co.uk
Twitter: @bookguild

Typeset in 11pt Minion Pro

Printed and bound by CPI Group (UK) Ltd, Croydon, CR0 4YY

ISBN 978 1913551 087

British Library Cataloguing in Publication Data.
A catalogue record for this book is available from the British Library.

To Nick, Claire, Martin, Maggie and Charlie.

To my former patients, staff and colleagues.

Your laughter was the best medicine of all.

Why I Wrote This Book

Since I retired, I have had the time to indulge in my hugely absorbing hobby of reading. I am an intrepid book lover, not a Kindle-worshipper but a real page-touching, page-turning lover of paperbacks. A true bibliophile. I have spent many a rainy afternoon (in the soggy Emerald Isle there are many) curled up happily with a book; always a biography or autobiography because I am intrigued – some may say nosey – by the lives of those people who allow me into their worlds and candidly divulge what makes them tick. Mostly, I am fond of those authors who deftly use phrases which are self-deprecating; those who can stand back and tell it how it is, often with a laconic, laidback lacing of humour, which only arrives with the wisdom of hindsight. I have read ALL the medical autobiographies that I have been able to get my hands on, so have entered the secret world of a brain surgeon, a general practitioner, a heart surgeon, a general surgeon, an intensive care doctor, a transplant surgeon, a nurse, a midwife, an air ambulance doctor, an airport doctor and even a prison doctor. I noticed that not one physiotherapist was willing (or brave enough) to provide an insight into their profession, so here goes. I hope to plug that gap with my take on the trials and tribulations of a career in physiotherapy and the many interesting, amusing and poignant anecdotes it has provided. I hope that you will enjoy reading it and, more importantly, that it makes you smile.

Chapter 1

The Interview

'Am I too small to be a physiotherapist?' I asked plaintively during my interview at The London Hospital School of Physiotherapy. I was sitting in a small, spartan office facing a formidable woman of about fifty with circular, thick-lensed spectacles, which gave her the look of a perspicacious wise owl as she perched intimidatingly behind a large wooden desk. I was just sixteen years of age and had previously been rejected by four other schools of physiotherapy in London. Guy's and St Thomas's had considered that I was too small to perform Cyriax manipulations, and The Middlesex and King's had rejected me for an undisclosed (possibly height-related) reason. No-one wanted little me. My timid question was answered immediately by Miss Orme, the formidable principal of The London Hospital School of Physiotherapy as she *descended* (yes, got down) from her elevated throne, to a height of well under five feet and corresponding girth, and shouted, 'I have never been too small for any aspect of physiotherapy.'

My mother brought the acceptance letter up to me in my bedroom and when I opened it, I whooped with joy and flung myself onto my bed with relief. 'Don't be silly,' my mother brusquely retorted, and so began a career in physiotherapy stretching fifty-seven years.

I had initially wanted to be a ballerina, but my controlling mother had insisted that I should have a career where I used my brain and not my body, so I had to give up my beloved ballet to study for O-levels. Then, I decided that I would like to teach games, as I quite liked the idea of playing sport at a high level while training at Bedford Physical Education College, and I was more than happy to perform the compulsory dance at the interview. However, this idea fizzled out the moment I broke my tibia and fibula (lower leg) when I was thrown from the pillion of a motorcycle in an accident sustained the first time I went out with a guy from the tennis club when I was sweet sixteen. It dawned on me that I had to be fit for my chosen profession. Oh, and I didn't much fancy having to shave my legs every day!

So, one Friday, I meekly trotted off to see Miss Balaam, my headmistress at Queen Elizabeth's Girls' Grammar School, Barnet, where I entered her hallowed office and timidly announced that I had decided not to train to be a sports mistress and could we discuss my possible options? There was no discussion; she just handed me a book on careers and said, 'Let me know what you want to do on Monday.' So much for career's advice in the 1950s! Miss Balaam was only interested in getting all her students to university. However, she did make an accurate prediction on one occasion, when she spoke to our year and announced that we would be the first year that would all get married AND have a career.

Panic set in! I liked the idea of medicine as a career but discounted it due to the five-year training. My mother suggested I spoke to Mr Jenkins, a partially sighted physiotherapist, who had a practice nearby. He showed me some of the weird apparatus and discussed the merits of physiotherapy as opposed to medicine. I ignored the comment of a physiotherapist being a doctor's handmaiden and the decision to do physiotherapy was entirely swung by the fact that the physiotherapy training only took three years. I had met my future husband (the guy with the motorbike) and did not want to wait five years before getting married. In those dark days, you were not allowed to get married while training and, more importantly, sex was strongly discouraged prior to wedlock in the days before the contraceptive pill.

On Monday morning, I knocked on Miss Balaam's sacred door and feebly announced that I would like to be a physiotherapist, even though I had no idea what it entailed. How daft was that! There was no suggestion of work experience or even physiotherapy departmental visits back then. How different it is nowadays, when students can chat to qualified physiotherapists and see if this profession, and all it has to offer, is the right fit for them.

In those days, it was possible to be accepted for physiotherapy training after O-levels, but I decided to stay on to sit for my A-levels. In any event, for some archaic reason, you had to be twenty-one years of age when you qualified as a physiotherapist. As it happened, I failed physics and chemistry and only passed zoology. I know now that I had not tested myself adequately when revising, but the fact that the whole class failed except for one brilliant student may have indicated a teaching problem.

Chapter 2

The London Hospital

The training course started in October 1959, so I travelled by tube from what the estate agents call 'the respectable area' of leafy Totteridge to Whitechapel Station and entered the deprived area of the East End of London. Whitechapel High Street was dirty and uninviting, littered with a profusion of higgledy-piggledy wooden stalls selling garments, fabrics and accoutrements from the 'Rag Trade'. This was the street where in 1888 Jack the Ripper murdered at least five prostitutes and mutilated their bodies. It was also the area where the notorious Kray Twins operated protection rackets, armed robberies and murders until they were convicted in 1969. We were advised to walk to the hospital opposite the station in twos, later on in threes. I mounted the steep stone steps of the imposing grey building of The London Hospital, which was constructed in the 1750s and badly in need of a wash and brush up (the building, not me!). Eventually, I found my way through a warren of underground corridors to the School of Physiotherapy, a building added later in 1936 to the rear of the hospital. This dingy environment was where I would spend my next three years.

I arrived feeling extremely small and very vulnerable, and was placed in a classroom of twenty students, where I met Meriel, who also knew no-one else, so whenever we needed a partner to massage, teach exercises to or experiment with the terrifying electrical equipment, we clung to each other like frightened limpets. Meriel was my best friend throughout the three-year training and then became one of my bridesmaids. She was beautiful, with a profusion of blonde hair, kindly blue eyes and a perfect hourglass figure. It was tragic that she died at a very young age from breast cancer. It was so sad. I miss her enormously. Still do.

My uniform consisted of six long white cotton overalls with bone buttons attached by scratchy metal shanks and a limp white cotton belt. On the first day, my overall came down to my ankles, so I had to traipse through the underground passages of the hospital to lunch looking ridiculous and hugely self-conscious. That night I hurriedly sewed up the hems to a fetching regulation mid-calf length! The rest of our uniform consisted of a dung-coloured blazer embroidered with The London Hospital badge, brown lace-up shoes, a hideous brown tie with a student tie pin sporting the hospital crest, six white aertex blouses and a brown serge exercise skirt with, you've guessed it, dung-coloured knickers! It is a wonder that any of us had a boyfriend!

We had to get changed in a cloakroom crammed with full-length metal lockers and open shelves for our smelly shoes with the barest amount of room to breathe (should we have wanted to). One time, I stood behind a colleague as she was spraying her hair with lacquer and I felt a sharp, disabling pain in my eye. A visit to casualty revealed a corneal ulcer, which fortunately healed after a few days with the eye ointment prescribed, but it warned me to take more care in future.

It was a strict regime. No eighteen-year-olds would cope with those harsh regulations today (and fortunately they don't have to). Our hair had to be up off our collar, so most of us had the then-stylish French pleat, heavily lacquered to stay in place all day. We had to have exceedingly short nails, no nail varnish, no jewellery and minimal make-up. If any of us had sported tattoos or piercings, we would have had our training swiftly terminated. We were inspected EVERY morning as we filed alphabetically past Miss Orme's room. In turn we would say, 'Good morning, Miss Orme,' which would be followed by an owl-like inspection and a reply of, 'Good morning, Miss Blundell,' and so on down the line. The girls at the front of the line would tear off their tie or tie pin and hand it to those further down the queue who had rushed in late.

We were all rather frightened of Miss Orme, who ruled her girls with an iron glove. We were the first year that grammar school pupils had been accepted for training, as previously only privileged girls from private education were admitted. Our training was relentless. We had only a four-week break in the summer and were envious of our friends at university who had longer holidays and who had a less regimented education. We were in an unnatural environment. Just girls. All virgins. Male students were not accepted then. When I wanted a day off to take my driving test (in case you are curious, I passed), I asked my father to telephone Miss Orme to say that I was unwell and would not be in. She was more amenable to requests from fathers rather than mothers. She would hold the door open for the consultants (mostly male in those days) while we questioned, 'Why?'

In the crowded classrooms, we received lessons in anatomy, physiology, massage, electrotherapy, exercises and movement.

We learned about all the diseases that afflicted the human race and as we were introduced to each one, we were sure that we had it too! Especially the fatal ones.

Our profession commenced in 1894 when four British nurses realised the value of massage for their patients and, in order to dissociate themselves from unscrupulous people offering massage as a euphemism for other services, formed The Chartered Society of Physiotherapy.

We learned the rudiments of massage so that we did not rub our patients up the wrong way or touch the out-of-bounds sensual areas. The wooden plinths were a standard height, so the smaller girls were given a massage platform to stand on. How I hated that platform, as it was a regular reminder of my short stature. We used talcum powder from a pepper pot kept in our pockets to provide an easy, gliding movement and combat our decidedly sweaty hands. We massaged the muscles of the face, neck, stomach, back, arms, legs and buttocks, being careful not to stray onto the forbidden upper third of the inner thigh. Effleurage (deep stroking) had to be performed towards the lymph glands in the groins and armpits to aid the lymphatic system and the flow of blood to the heart. Abdominal massage was used for the relief of constipation and blocked wind. Always a delight! Back and neck massage were used for relaxing tight musculature and relieving pain. We learned techniques such as kneading (circular movements), petrissage (finger kneading), rolling, hacking and clapping. We practised on our partners and always volunteered to be the model for the last session of the day, when we would not have to leap up and concentrate on yet another critical lecture. When we had an internal examination (not what you think!), we had to massage Miss Orme's arm until she was covered in a haze of talcum powder.

In electrotherapy classes we copied our notes from the blackboard word for word. How mind-numbing is that! We learned about direct current, alternating current, shortwave diathermy (deep heat), infrared (heat) and ultraviolet (sunlight) treatments. We had to learn, understand and draw the electrical circuits of all the apparatus that we used. We could have been employed as electricians (with greater earning potential).

It was during an electrotherapy lecture, in a small, spartan classroom where an electrical circuit had been drawn on a chalky blackboard, that my friend Anne told me that she had had an abortion the previous day. I am surprised that I can even remember what the lecture was about – we were learning about the direction of the current, I think – because I was so shocked by this flash of electrifying and explosive news. I wanted to hear about it there and then, but instead had to listen to the lecturer, a spinster in her fifties, drone on and on. I pretended to be interested while stealing glances at Anne as she sat quietly, her hands in her lap, looking down at the tissue she was holding, keeping herself together, just.

Afterwards, while we had a coffee, she told me all about it. We sat in a corner, hunched over our drinks, as she explained she had returned pregnant from a camping holiday in France with her boyfriend. She was distraught at having to make such a ghastly decision, but she felt there was no way she could have continued with her studies, being pregnant and then a mother, so decided to seek out a backstreet abortion from a nurse, who used a knitting needle. Abortion was illegal in the UK until the Abortion Act of 1968 made it legal for women up to twenty-eight weeks' gestation, so if she wanted to be a physiotherapist – and she did – she would have no choice. The contraceptive pill wasn't introduced until 1961 in the UK, and then only on prescription to married women. Girls like Anne at the time were often faced with stark choices like these. Being an unmarried mother and a student – never mind a go-to-work mum – were unthinkable in the society that we lived in during the 1960s.

Anne told me about the finer, more painful details of her abortion: how she sat bleeding, doubled in pain, alone and miserable on the toilet of her family home, glad that her parents were out for the evening, on a sad rainy night, while her body expelled the foetus and the wind howled outside. I wondered how many students would have to give up their careers because of unplanned pregnancies. It was shame enough, at the time, to get caught having sex outside marriage, never mind getting pregnant.

I was determined that this would not happen to me, as my mother had instilled in me that if I became pregnant, I would be sent away to the country to have the baby, who would then be adopted. She would have preferred to send a grandchild away rather than face a disapproving society, and she was a pillar of the church, who, surely, in that role should have been understanding and forgiving. I knew instances of this callous disregard for the poor girls who had been unlucky and caught out, and how they had been treated so cruelly. In the sixties, there was no regard for the lifelong psychological trauma inflicted on the young mothers, whose babies had been wrenched from them or indeed for the children themselves who were often unaware of the reason for their adoption and suffered from a loss of identity and, in the majority of cases, an inability to trace their biological parents.

Later, Anne's abortion resulted in a serious pelvic infection and she was admitted to the gynaecological ward by Miss Orme, who demonstrated a previously unseen and caring side. She was lucky. Before 1968, women who had no choice but to seek a backstreet abortion would risk excessive bleeding, infection, damage to their internal organs and even death at the hands of unqualified abortionists.

I wonder how many girls that Miss Orme cared for in a similar way. She must have known that she could lose her star pupils –

and the NHS would lose some fine physiotherapists – if she didn't do this for them. It strikes me that this was an amazingly broad-minded and brave thing for her to do at the time.

Anne never had children due to the abortion, which was a source of great pain to her, even though she went on to be a most accomplished and empathetic physiotherapist.

Not all the electrotherapy lectures were so distressing, and training continued in the soulless classrooms. I caught up and learned that the main electrotherapy unit was the faradic battery, which made the muscles contract when two electrodes placed inside damp pads were applied to the skin. These pads had to be folded accurately so that there were sixteen sides of lint. Faradism (after Michael Faraday 1791–1867) was used to teach patients how to contract their muscles so that they could exercise in the right way. We had an antique, polished mahogany box with a dial on top for the intensity of the current and a cylindrical iron core the size of a stick of rock, which we slid in and out of a hole in the side of the box (in a rather suggestive way) to surge the current. It was most uncomfortable, but we students were young and pretty then, and our patients returned for more! It was used mainly for stimulating weak quadriceps (thigh muscles) for patients who had difficulty in walking. It was also quite successful for stimulating the little muscles of the arches of the foot for folk with flat or painful feet.

Horrifyingly, we used alternating sinusoidal current in a Schnee four-cell bath for poor circulation before this treatment was rendered obsolete. The patient would sit with each foot in a deep leg bath filled with water while zinc electrodes would deliver the current. Patients were very apprehensive and needed reassuring that it was therapeutic to mix electricity and water (while we wondered too!).

We used direct current for giving Renotin gel ionisations to deliver this derivative of histamine into painful areas such as tennis elbow and golfer's elbow, and had to remember whether we placed the active pad smeared in gel over the positive or negative electrode to force this counter-irritant into the skin. Don't ask me which, it was sixty years ago! Now, mercifully, cortisone injections have superseded this complex treatment. Also, we used hideous nasal ionisations with two wires covered in lint pushed up the nose for hayfever in the days before anti-allergy medication such as Piriton came on the market.

I treated a young girl who had Bell's palsy, a disfiguring paralysis of the facial muscles, which caused her face to droop on one side, while the corresponding eyelid failed to close and her mouth dribbled saliva. It had been particularly distressing for her to wake up with a lopsided smile. This frightening condition is believed to be caused by either pressure on the facial nerve or by a viral infection. I applied a damp padded disc to each facial muscle on the affected side and stimulated the muscle directly with intermittent direct current, thus getting the muscle to twitch. This treatment is not used today. Now, the treatment of choice is the steroid prednisolone, which should be administered within seventy-two hours of the symptoms appearing in order to reduce inflammation. A soft patch may be provided to protect the eye and prevent irritating soreness. Also, gentle exercises may be performed as the condition improves. Most patients begin to get better after two weeks and happily return to normal function within three to six months.

We treated patients in dusty curtained cubicles. One time, I switched off a plug on the wall behind the curtains so that I could use the socket for my piece of equipment. There was a startled YELP, like you hear from a dog whose tail has been shut in the door, so I quickly switched it back on again, which caused another YELP, but considerably louder. I had inadvertently switched off the direct current used for a Renotin ionisation in the next-door cubicle and given the poor lady a couple of very unpleasant shocks. I apologised to the physio student and to the dear lady, and fortunately was not reprimanded for my mistake, but it taught me a lesson which I will never forget.

At The London, deep heat was delivered by a shortwave diathermy machine, which had two dark brown saucer-sized bakelite electrodes, each attached to a moveable arm which was jointed like an angle-poise lamp. Each joint was controlled by a wing nut (which regularly fell off), so we had difficulty trying to adjust the arms in order to position the electrodes either side of the joint needing treatment, making sure it did not come into contact with the skin. The austere wooden cubicle was lined with a hideous metal cage designed to prevent interference with radio waves during the war. We were surprised that fifteen years after the war, the cage had not been dismantled. Perhaps the hospital was anticipating another war or just thought it was an unnecessary job. Either way, it was rather claustrophobic and certainly was not aesthetically pleasing to our patients or to us.

Years later, in another hospital, the shortwave machine was situated in a physio department next to the manager's office and blocked his phone every time it was used, which must have been maddening for him, but it demonstrated to us the ability of electromagnetic waves to penetrate through a wall. We used this treatment to provide deep heat for painful joints such as shoulders, knees and hips, usually from the ravages of osteoarthritis. We had to make sure that there was no metal in the field of the energy waves, which would concentrate the current and cause a burn (similar to a microwave oven), so patients had to bare the area being treated. There was also a long, black coil, rather like a snake, which had a mind of its own, that we had to wind carefully round patients' knees using spacers so that one part of the coil did not touch another part and cause overheating. This was an art form in itself and happily is no longer used.

Superficial heat was delivered by an infrared luminous lamp or a non-luminous element with a large, imposing metal lampshade, which was positioned over our patients to relax their muscles and ease pain. I was treating a man with back pain once when the large glass bulb EXPLODED over his bare back and I had to pick out hot shards of glass from his skin. There was no guard on the lamp back then. Fortunately, my patient did not complain. Perhaps he dined out on the tale. Who knows? Patients seemed to enjoy being at the mercy of young, female students. In fact, he thanked me warmly and made me a coffee table, which I duly took home on the Tube.

The NHS, started in 1948, was in its infancy when I commenced my physiotherapy training in 1959. Patients were delighted to be treated free. As they are today. The Health and Safety at Work Act in 1974 was light years away and patient safety was not then deemed to be a priority. The only caution that I can remember was that we had to lock up the methylated spirit that we used to clean the skin in case the furtive alcoholics nicked it!

For ultraviolet light (sunlight) treatment, we had to warm up the lamp first, then measure the distance from the patient and calculate the allotted time, which was progressed for each treatment. We wore goggles, as did our patients, who had to strip while they received treatment for skin conditions such as acne and psoriasis. We knew about the danger of sunlight to the cornea of the eye but were unaware that our lamps could cause serious skin cancer.

We also had a Kromayer lamp, the shape of a hairdryer, which projected a beam of ultraviolet light the size of a 50p piece down either side of our patients' spines as a counter-irritant for pain. The idea was that superficial skin soreness would block the deep pain in the joints! This archaic treatment left a series of burnt brown circles down our patients' backs, which were clearly visible to their next of kin when they arrived home. One lady I was treating mentioned that a child had shouted to her friends when she went swimming, 'Look at those horrid marks on that woman's back.' Later in my career, long after this treatment was thankfully abandoned, I treated an Egyptian gentleman who had a series of ugly T-shaped burn marks all down the back of his leg from branding irons as treatment in Egypt for his sciatica.

We had a wax bath filled with liquid paraffin wax which was used to dip patients' hands or feet in four or five times in order to build up a thick coating of warm wax which resembled a glove or bootie to soothe painful hands or feet. After twenty minutes of treatment the wax covering was peeled off, sterilised and returned to the bath. It was NOT like the depilatory wax that elicits a hair-raising scream and a death message to the therapist at beauty salons! This was the days before women asked for a 'Brazilian' and men requested a 'Back, Sack and Crack'!

At The London we had a hydrotherapy pool, where we would don a regulation navy-blue costume (no, it didn't have arms and legs, but I like the way you are thinking!) and accompany our patients into the pool. Patients were treated for osteoarthritic joints, after a stroke and for a variety of neurological conditions. They were floated with various buoyancy aids and encouraged to exercise in the warm water. Patients loved their hydrotherapy sessions.

For the first six months we spent most days in the classroom or gymnasium being drummed with the theory and practice of physiotherapeutic techniques before we were let loose on patients.

It was most welcome to leave the classroom and visit the other departments of the hospital. Our training included two weeks' nursing in order to understand the roles of the nurses that we would be working alongside. I was placed for this duty with Jeanine, who had a wonderful sense of humour and became a firm friend. We also had to work a night duty to appreciate the role of the nurses, which we both found extraordinarily tiring. I remember we had to tiptoe round the eye ward as patients, who had undergone cataract surgery, had BOTH eyes completely covered and had to lie in bed quietly for weeks. How very different from the treatment today when patients leave hospital the same day.

On the male chest ward, many patients were smokers and suffered from chest infections such as pneumonia and tuberculosis. Cancer wasn't mentioned. They were encouraged to cough and spit into half-pint metal pots in order to clear their chest of the infected secretions. The worst thing that I did on this ward was to drop a full sputum pot onto the floor with a BANG. Everyone stared. I can still see the mess now as it was so unpleasant – nay, impossible – to clear up. Apart from that incident, I thoroughly enjoyed my time caring for the patients and could easily have switched to the nursing profession, apart from the nights! My nocturnal/diurnal rhythm would never have recovered.

After six months, one of our set, who had passed chemistry, physics and zoology at A-level, went to see Miss Orme and asked if she could transfer to the medical college. When I heard that Miss Orme had kindly arranged this for her, I was envious and would have asked too, had I not flunked two of my A-levels. It seemed as if I was destined to be a physiotherapist, though I still secretly hankered after becoming a doctor.

We had visits to the revered medical college and viewed the musculature of cadavers, which were preserved in formalin. The smell was overpowering and hit you as you walked in. Once inside, we considered it was exceedingly thoughtful that these kind people had bequeathed their bodies to medical science and gave them the utmost respect. It was helpful to see each of the muscles in situ and I would have loved to have been able to have joined the medical students and done some dissection. After all, at school I had received a 'Distinguished Work' for a dogfish dissection! At the end of term when Miss Balaam read out my contribution to the 'Distinguished Works', the whole school erupted and roared with laughter. So much for my greatest achievement!

I was fascinated by the anatomy of the human body and wanted to explore the muscles, tendons and joints in more detail. We followed the contours of the muscles when we did surface anatomy, but I would have liked to be allowed to cut and demonstrate the deeper layers of the body. I wanted to see where each muscle originated and where it was inserted. Later in my career, I visited the anatomy department of Bristol University to investigate the configuration of the male pelvic floor muscles. The anatomist there was unable to show me the separate muscles due to the fact that, unfortunately, humans die with their legs together. In frustration, I drew the muscles on the blackboard and showed him exactly what I was trying to find. He had no knowledge of any of these important muscles.

When I was training, it would have been useful to watch the enhanced muscles of the contestants in the Mr Universe Contest, but that did not start until 1965. The first female bodybuilding contest did not begin until even later in 1977.

Much later in 1995, I heard about the Body Worlds exhibition brought to London by Dr Gunther von Hagen, who used human bodies from donors after they had given express permission for their corpse to be used in this way. He found a way of revealing the skeleton with the muscles preserved in red plastic. It was fascinating. At this exhibition, I was examining the male pelvic floor muscles by bending down and looking up the male model when a steward came across and asked me what I was doing. He must have thought that I was rather sexually motivated until I informed him that I was a PhD student studying the male pelvic floor muscles!

Later, I found it useful to have a knowledge of anatomy when I was indulging in my newfound hobby of sculpture. I thought about the musculature while I was modelling the clay, before sending the sculptures to the foundry to be cast in bronze for posterity.

We also visited the pathology laboratory and were introduced to the fascinating way that bugs spread ferociously on agar jelly in a petri dish and the absence of bugs where the jelly contained the correct antibiotic. While I was in the lab, I performed a unique test to identify my own blood group, where I learned that I was AB positive, a 'universal recipient', which is quite handy.

While I was at The London, we were allowed to watch surgical operations. The first operation that I chose to watch was a thyroid operation. The patient was already anaesthetised and lying on his back before the surgeon took a scalpel and cut the skin across this man's throat. I saw no more. I quickly left the room as I felt decidedly faint.

Later, I felt similarly light-headed when I watched my son have the skin on his eyebrow stitched up by a young doctor, who had obviously missed out on needlework lessons. The last thing that I saw was the catgut thread become tangled and when I came to, I was sitting on a chair with my head between my knees. I did wonder if I had the bottle to perform surgery. Would I have been able to cut and repair without fainting?

I was brave enough to watch a heart operation. I found that if I was sitting down I wouldn't go 'woozy', so I sat in the visitor's gallery of the imposing wood-panelled theatre with interested students from all the disciplines. We were told that the surgeon could only stop the heart for FOUR MINUTES without compromising the blood supply to the brain, providing the patient's body was cooled with ice, so while we were watching the heart valve being expertly repaired, we anxiously watched the second hand of the large ticking clock. Now, surgery has developed exponentially with the introduction of the heart/lung machine, so surgeons can perform more complex cases, such as valve replacement, bypass surgery and even heart transplants.

I was also invited to watch the birth of a baby boy just as the crown of his head appeared to the outside world. It was brilliant to witness this miracle of nature, which made birth seem so easy and natural (thankfully, I had been spared watching the mother in labour).

We visited the London Hospital Museum and saw many fascinating freak exhibits preserved for posterity in a selection of glass jars of different sizes (it is a wonder that so many of the human race are normal). The star exhibit was the skeleton of Joseph Merrick, the Elephant Man. We saw his skull, which was hideously enlarged and misshapen from multiple bony protuberances, and also the black hood that he wore over his head, and were horrified to learn how this poor man had lived his later life in the Whitechapel area, only venturing out at night.

The museum included two pieces of obsolete physiotherapy equipment: firstly, the longwave diathermy deep heat machine, which was replaced by shortwave, and secondly, the carbon arc lamp which was replaced by the modern ultraviolet lamp. We saw pictures of East End children, who were not exposed naturally to sunshine, wearing just goggles and underpants, sitting round the carbon arc lamp as a prevention for rickets.

In the museum we saw the large bell that was rung in The London Hospital when extra staff were needed to hold down a patient in the operating room for surgery, such as amputations, in the days before anaesthesia. How gruesome was that!

The physiotherapy training was exhausting. We were given weekly theory tests in each physiotherapy subject and were told that we would have to leave the course if we failed any of them.

I travelled every day by tube from Woodside Park Station on the Northern Line, changing at Bank Station, then on to the District Line to Whitechapel Station, a tiring journey, taking one and a half hours each way. Occasionally on the way home, I fell asleep and landed up at High Barnet where the Northern Line terminated! It was an exhausting training made worse by having homework every evening in preparation for the dreaded weekly tests.

I asked my mother to let me live in the halls of residence so that I would not have such a tiring journey, but she refused my pleas, even though my sister had stayed in halls while she was at teacher training college. Mother was a teacher and the disciplinarian in our family. It was useless to argue with her.

We were taught about every bone in the body and where the muscles attached from their origin to their insertion. We drew all the bones, joints and ligaments. We became expert in posture, body movement and gait analysis. We drew pin men and added the muscles necessary to show different ways of moving. I brought human bones home on the Tube to study at home, which I am not sure was allowed (I never asked). Nowadays, students have plastic bones and skeletons to study, hopefully made from recycled plastic.

We were taught Proprioceptive Neuromuscular Facilitation (PNF), a form of strengthening our patient's muscles as if our life depended on it. Don't ask! (See the glossary, if you must.) We had to stretch our patients' arms or legs and then use force to push against their active movements. We became exceedingly fit – nay, muscle-bound – as we demonstrated a range of explosive techniques.

We learned how to take exercise classes, how to project our voice and use commands, how to enthuse our patients and encourage greater effort, and, most importantly, how to always praise their achievements.

We retained our femininity by wearing pretty-coloured matching bras, pants and waist petticoats, and became immune to stripping off for all the practical classes. Our pastel petticoats became blackened from travelling by Underground, so we ditched the subtle colours and wore sexy black underwear. When I blew my nose, the tissue would reveal black nasal mucus, the same colour as the secretions in my lungs (and I was not a smoker). I expect it is still like this for travellers in the Underground today.

We went on to the wards with a more senior student and shadowed them. I shall never forget the horror of watching my mentor make a young lad with severe burns over most of his torso stretch his arms upwards. I had never seen a burns patient before. I couldn't cope with watching this poor chap in agony as his scar tissue stretched, bled and suppurated. I felt for him. 'Are you OK?' my mentor asked me afterwards. 'You are white as a sheet.' I was not alright. I thought that I would never be able to make a young lad suffer in this way. Much later, I learned that patients could have their pain relief medication timed to be effective before physiotherapy treatment, which was expected to be uncomfortable.

We learned to be carers. We also learned not to offend our patients, sometimes the hard way. One lady with rheumatoid arthritis said to me, 'What lovely hands you have.' to which I shrugged and said, 'No, I don't think so.' She then placed her horrendously deformed hands on the table for treatment and I could have cut out my tongue with embarrassment. A stark lesson. I can remember assisting a dear little old lady to walk. She had severe osteoarthritis and as I supported her I could hear and feel her joints creaking loudly, due to the noise of bone end on bone end where she had lost the cartilage cushions in the days before joint replacement surgery. We became empathetic with patients in pain. It felt good to be able to reduce discomfort and assist people to move. I loved treating patients. It was a privilege to be able to help. It was when I was helping patients that I knew I had chosen the right profession.

We were advised not to talk to our patients about religion, politics or sex. We learned quite quickly that you did not say to men, 'Hop up on the bed and I will be with you in a minute.' Indeed, one time I said, 'Hop up on the bed,' and he did exactly that! Another time I said to a patient, 'How do you feel?' and he replied, 'With my hands.'

We learned to be respectful and cover our patients adequately so that only the part to be treated was exposed. We were advised to stay with our patients while they were having treatments such as cervical or lumbar traction, shortwave diathermy or slings.

Once, I found it almost impossible to stay anywhere near a female patient whose legs I had suspended in slings to increase the range of abduction in her hips. Every time she parted her legs there was a ghastly unwashed smell. And my sense of smell is poor! That was the only time that I nearly gagged in the whole of my career.

I could always tell which patients smoked when they removed their clothes and the cubicle would be filled with stale smoke, which was thoroughly unpleasant, not just for me, but for the next few patients too. Smoking increased dramatically during the war, mainly due to the policy of providing free cigarettes to allied troops as a morale-boosting exercise. The knowledge that smoking caused a range of serious diseases was only confirmed in the 1950s and 1960s after a series of major medical reports. As a young physiotherapist, I felt unable to advise patients to quit smoking, but much later, when I undertook my research, I offered the smokers a 'Smoking Cessation Programme.'

At eighteen months into the course, we tentatively took external written preliminary examinations of The Chartered Society of Physiotherapy at the scary examination hall in London. We had papers in anatomy and physiology, electrotherapy and exercises. Going to a specified building took us out of our comfort zone, and it would have been altogether kinder to let us sit the examination in our own hospital. I have since found one of the examination papers in anatomy and physiology, and wondered how I had passed!

Dear reader, if you are non-medical or allergic to exams, please don't bother to read these two papers. I don't want you to be bored this early on.

PRELIMINARY EXAMINATION

Anatomy and Physiology

PAPER A
(Three hours allowed)

Four questions to be answered.
1. Give an account of the quadriceps femoris muscle. State how you would demonstrate the various parts of this muscle.
2. Describe the movements of the thoracic cage and diaphragm during respiration.
3. Give a brief description of the pituitary gland and describe **three** of its functions.
4. Describe the arrangement of a synovial sheath. Give an account of the synovial sheaths found on the flexor aspect of the wrist and hand.
5. Describe the origin, course and distribution of the obturator nerve.
6. Write notes on each of the following:
    a. Plasma proteins;
    b. Extra pyramidal system;
    c. Gastric juice.

I answered (attempted) 1, 2, 4 and 5. As if that wasn't enough, the next day there was more.

Anatomy and Physiology

Paper B
(Three hours allowed)

Four questions to be answered. Two from each section.
  Section 1
  1. Give an account of the structure of a nerve fibre and discuss the functions of the fibres of a typical spinal nerve.
  2. Describe the movements that occur at the hip joint. How may range of movement be tested?
  3. Describe the venous drainage of the lower limb and discuss the factors influencing venous return from the leg to the heart.

  Section 2
  4. Write an account of the characteristics of the red blood corpuscles.
  5. Write an account of the factors which influence growth and calcification of bones.
  6. Explain the mechanisms which maintain the temperature of the body within fairly narrow limits.

I answered questions 2, 3, 4 and 6.

At two and a half years into the course, we were exposed to The Chartered Society of Physiotherapy's external written intermediate examinations, which covered a variety of patient conditions and the possible treatments. Again, we nervously assembled at the foreboding examination hall in London.

After passing these essential exams, for the next six months we spent ALL DAY treating patients under supervision and felt that we were unpaid labour, as nurses were paid during their training while we paid out for ours (albeit, in most cases, with a government grant). Finals were entirely practical, using the innocent first-year students as our models.

Surprisingly, the examiner allocated for my final examination was Mr Jenkins, the man who persuaded me to train as a physiotherapist, and even though he failed to recognise me due to his poor eyesight, I asked for another examiner to avoid any bias, otherwise I would never have considered that I had passed on my own merit.

I was asked to give the unsuspecting student a Renotin ionisation to her right tennis elbow. I collected the jar of gel, spatula, electrodes, leads, lint and bandage on a tray. I folded the pads then unscrewed the jar of gel. Horror of horrors, it was not a gel but a kind of liquid paste which oozed out menacingly and completely surrounded all of the items on my tray. What a mess! Meekly, I mentioned to the examiner that our Renotin was a stiff gel, so she said kindly, 'Why don't you start again?' Gratefully, I did. I set up another tray then put the liquid slosh on the pad, placed in over the outside of the right elbow under the positive electrode, then placed the indifferent pad and electrode on the inside of her elbow and bandaged them firmly on. I set the machine to deliver direct current, asked my model if it was comfortable and slowly increased the intensity. Despite my first messy tray, I must have got the correct electrode because I managed to pass.

Our strict training at The London must have been second to none, as one of our set, Rocca Herd, won the National Award for being the best physiotherapy student in the 1962 Chartered Society of Physiotherapy final exams, and she was the shortest student! Miss Orme was beside herself with pride. I think she took all the credit herself! Standards were paramount to her and this award indicated the exacting standard to which we had all been drilled. Sadly, Rocca died recently from pancreatic cancer. She was a brilliant student and had a charmed career. I miss her and her amazing zest for life. I was honoured to be asked to give her eulogy and I hope that I captured the essence of this awesomely impressive physiotherapist. It was a very sad day.

Happily, fifteen out of the intake of twenty passed their finals (four dropped out from the course and one girl retook finals six months later) and we became members of The Chartered Society of Physiotherapy and received a diploma and crested badge from The London Hospital. We had an award ceremony to which we could invite only one guest, which I thought was rather unfair. Would I invite my new husband or my mother? After much thought, I invited my mother, as she had encouraged me to train as a physiotherapist.

In 1990, The London Hospital became The Royal London Hospital. When I retired I donated my certificate and badge to The Royal London Hospital Museum, as they did not have either of them on display in their new museum. If any reader has hung on to their brown blazer and skirt, the museum would be delighted to receive them. They must be the only folk who want them! They were not so keen on the mud-coloured knickers.

When I received the good news that I had passed, Miss Orme asked if I would like to stay on and work at The London Hospital (which was considered a great honour), so I informed her that this was impossible as I was getting married in three weeks. 'Getting married, Miss Blundell!' she shrieked. She was clearly shocked by my announcement and quite unable to say 'Congratulations'.

I was getting married as soon as I could. I desperately wanted to leave home and make my own decisions. I was twenty-two and still sharing a bedroom with my sister. My mother was very strict and dictatorial, and I was ready to live my own life. Oh! and unsurprisingly I wanted to have sexual relations with the handsome man I loved.

In the three weeks that I had available to make my wedding dress, I did not leave the house. London was bathed in a yellow smog called a 'pea-souper', despite the Clean Air Act of 1956 prohibiting dark smoke from chimneys, in response to the Great London Smog of 1952. Fortunately, the smog lifted the day before my wedding, so guests could travel safely to the church in Totteridge and importantly, the wedding party would be visible in the photographs. Photographs were black and white then and only taken outside in good light by a professional photographer with an antique wooden tripod, who covered his head in a black cloth as he peered through the screen, and when everyone said 'cheese', he squeezed a rubber ball and the negative mysteriously appeared on a large plate! He then went back to his studio to develop the photographs, which were ceremoniously brought round the next day. If one paid a little extra, the photos could be professionally tinted.

Chapter 3

Harrow Hospital

On 15th December 1962, I married Tony Dorey in a white wedding dress with white fox fur round the hem in St Andrew's Parish Church in Totteridge and became Mrs Dorey. He had been the love of my life for six long years. My sister Joyce and best friend Meriel were bridesmaids and looked stunning in African violet satin dresses with satin shoes dyed to match, while my young cousin Claire was a cute child bridesmaid resplendent in lilac chiffon. Quite by accident rather than design, the colours blended beautifully with the purple altar cloth. Perfect co-ordination and the start of a bright future.

The reception was held in the Red Lion at Barnet, where the very next day the plaster ceiling fell down! I cannot believe that our sedate reception was the cause, as evening dances were unheard of back then. Tony and I spent a week on honeymoon at the Grand Hotel in Torquay where we had a tasteful room, but we had to go down a long corridor to the bathroom with a sponge bag under one arm and hope that it was vacant when we got there. It was only when holidaymakers started taking package deals abroad that they demanded en-suite accommodation in the UK. We made love once on honeymoon and when I wanted more, I was called a nymphomaniac! I refused to go on the pill before I had a family, as we did not know then if it would affect future offspring, so we used a condom. Just the one!

In January 1963 I started work at Harrow Physical Treatment Centre. It was the year of the severe winter so, after pushing my new husband's car off in the deep snow, I walked to work in Wellington boots carrying my flat shoes. I strongly disliked arriving at the stark, unwelcoming building, situated in a rundown car park in the middle of Harrow. It was a most foreboding place with the sort of high windows only found in a prison cell, as it had been a gas decontamination centre during the war. Miss Locke (aged about one hundred) was the superintendent physiotherapist, but some of her staff were unqualified and allowed to treat patients due to a (daft) post-war rule. All the physiotherapists were elderly apart from Dorothy, who became my friend and confidante. She had a delightful sense of the ridiculous and we laughed about the archaic regime that had probably been in existence since the Middle Ages. I worked full-time, including two evening clinics a week, and received an unremarkable £10 per week (before tax).

The doctor of physical medicine prescribed the necessary treatment: e.g. shortwave and exercises to the right hip, three times a week for four weeks. He would then review the patient. If the patient twisted their ankle on the way to the clinic, we were not allowed to treat the recent injury until they had a new referral. How daft was that! I hated this prescriptive stranglehold and desperately wanted my own autonomy. Patients were allocated by a senior member of staff each time they arrived, so there was no continuity of care. Female patients were treated in one room while male patients were treated in the other. The male patients were treated by male physios and I had to ask repeatedly if I could also treat the men. Eventually as a concession, I was allowed to treat the men in the evenings.

While I was at the dingy treatment centre, one of the unqualified physios forgot a patient, who was meant to be under the ultraviolet lamp for just a few minutes, when she went off to have her lunch. When she returned and realised her ghastly mistake, the doctor was informed, but fortunately the patient was not severely sunburnt. There was no reaction. Nothing. The lamp had not been tested in years!

One of the elderly physios, who had trained as a remedial gymnast, used to suspend her patients from the wall bars in the gym, hanging by their hands to give traction to their spines. Also, she used to give her back patients the 'medicine ball treatment' if she considered them to be malingering. She made them lift this heavy ball up from outstretched arms while lying face down. Her patients only came once.

Any visitor to the gym would think that they had walked into a badly lit mediaeval torture chamber. At any time, there would be patients hanging round the walls by their fingertips, folk with limbs suspended in slings struggling to move, people strapped down on the traction 'rack', and one or two guys moaning under the weight of the killer medicine ball. All at the mercy of a controlling grey-haired remedial therapy misandrist.

When I was in the gym, one of my patients appeared with a hot swollen calf muscle which was indicative of a deep vein thrombosis. I reported this to the doctor, who rather arrogantly thought it was astounding that a young physio could diagnose such a condition! To me this was only part of our rigorous training and I failed to understand why he was so surprised.

After six months, I asked if I could transfer to Harrow Hospital as I found the physical treatment centre too depressing and claustrophobic, and wanted freedom to work on the orthopaedic wards. Happily, this was granted, and I stayed there until we moved house to Chesham in 1964.

In the hospital, I was helping a lady to walk up the stairs when she collapsed. I shouted for help, but no sound came out. Not a peep. It was the first time that I realised how shock could affect me. I had never lost my voice before (or since). Eventually, another member of staff came past and we managed to get her back into bed. She had sustained a mini-stroke and fortunately she recovered.

On the wards, the consultants gave explicit instructions for their patients, e.g. for patients lying in bed for up to three months with their broken thigh on traction: 'Breathing exercises and anti-thrombosis leg exercises'; or after several weeks when their femur had healed: 'Non-weight-bearing, and stairs'. How much better treatment is for those patients with fractured femurs now; they are pinned or have a hip replacement and can be up and walk the next day.

If I was asked to help a very tall man to walk with crutches and I came up to his navel, I would ask a porter to help me (physiotherapy helpers weren't invented then). Otherwise, the patient would be frightened that I was too small to support him adequately and for me, it would be like trying to stop a ladder from wobbling by just holding on to the bottom rung!

Chapter 4

West Herts Hospital

When we moved to Chesham, I applied for a basic grade post at West Herts Hospital, Hemel Hempstead. I needed a car to be able to get to work, so my brother sold me his maroon Austin Cambridge (circa 1954) for £30. It was not a pretty car. It resembled a bomb and had many drawbacks. Importantly, I needed to sit on a cushion so that I could see over the steering wheel. I was told that there was an egg in the radiator to prevent further leaks; it needed a clothes peg on the choke to hold it open (and a good memory to remember to remove it after two miles); and the driver's semaphore indicator, which sprung up impressively, needed to be cancelled by unwinding the window by hand and ramming it back into the door pillar. The worst problem was its refusal to start. It needed to be wound up with a starting handle or bump started. Fortunately, I lived on a hill and worked at a hospital on a hill, so I could bump start it with alacrity. The difficulty was trying to find a garage situated on a hill that gave out quadruple Green Shield stamps! If I went shopping and parked it on a flat piece of road, when I wanted to leave I would confidently place the starting handle in the hole in the front of the car and pretend to wind it. This would bring men running to my aid to prove their superior strength. It never failed! Oh, the benefits of youth!

At West Herts, the physiotherapy receptionist gave us our own patients, which was a huge leap forward. Once, I was given a sweet little nun of decidedly diminutive stature to treat because the receptionist said that I was nearest to her height! She couldn't even see over the reception desk. I used a series of stools to form a staircase to help her onto the couch. Her knees were giving her trouble from all the kneeling that was expected at the nunnery. While I was treating her, she confided in me that she had been persuaded to become a nun by her mother because she had no vagina. Bless her. The prevalence of female congenital pelvic malformations is two to four per cent. Today, now surgery has advanced, it is often possible to fashion a vagina in many of these disadvantaged patients.

I asked Eileen, the friendly receptionist, to give me all the young men, whom I had enjoyed treating, when they came back for follow-up treatment. I even marked their treatment cards with a cross in the top right-hand corner. Fifty years later, she told me how she smiled when these old men with a cross on the corner of their treatment cards slowly staggered in!

One time, I was given a gentleman to treat who had been verbally abusive to three other physiotherapy staff. Now it was my turn. I sat next to him on the plinth and asked him why three physios had refused to treat him, whereupon he burst into tears and told me that his wife had just died and that life was shitty. I sympathised and afterwards he became an exceptionally good-natured and amenable patient, and I received a lesson on the importance of understanding the patient as a whole.

At West Herts we used the ultraviolet light Kromayer to treat wounds, either directly to the wound or with an array of different-shaped clear glass applicators to slide into sinuses so that the wounds would heal from the base upwards. One day, I was treating a delightful lady with ultraviolet light to a deep wound on her foot. I spread Vaseline around the edges of the area and illuminated the wound. Within a minute the machine EXPLODED with an almighty BANG and flames started licking round the casing. I swiftly unplugged the apparatus and, not so calmly, wheeled the Kromayer out of the rear of the wooden building and onto the path. Apparently, the cause of this explosion was due to the fact that no-one had filled the machine with water to cool it. Fortunately, this was not my duty.

I was only reprimanded once. I was treating a patient in a curtained cubicle when a spider the size of a dinner plate descended from the wooden beam right in front of my nose. I SCREAMED. The physiotherapy superintendent felt that I was being extremely unprofessional! That said, I would probably react in the same way today, only louder. Later when I joined BUPA, I telephoned the porter to come and remove a large spider which was dangling in the doorway, blocking my exit and prevented me from going home. Two porters came to my aid, possibly to either view this gargantuan arachnid or maybe just to hold each other's hand.

It was at West Herts when I realised that we needed Continuing Professional Development. Up till then I had only used the treatments that I had been taught while training. Research was in its infancy and gradually some of the treatments became obsolete and were destined for the annals of history. The Schnee four-cell bath was one victim, mainly because it was a pain filling the deep leg baths with warm water! Cortisone injections eliminated the need for Renotin ionisations. Yippee!

We still used nasal ionisations for hayfever and we still used faradism with the SAME zinc electrode for BOTH urinary and faecal incontinence! Before the days of Health and Safety, and Infection Control, the electrodes were washed and placed all together in a jam jar of water! Fortunately, now we have single-patient electrodes.

We also performed nerve conduction tests and plotted graphs to indicate the speed at which impulses travelled along a nerve. This helped to work out how the nerves were functioning and their ability to send impulses to the muscles. They were useful in diagnosing disorders such as hysterical palsy, where the problem was brain-centred and not nerve-related, or, on the other hand, if there was a genuine blockage of nerve fibres, as in carpal tunnel syndrome, where the nerve was squashed by the bones in the wrist.

I joined The Chiltern Group of physiotherapists and was asked to organise a manipulation course at Wendover by the excellent tutor, John Challoner. Almost immediately the course was filled with twenty keen physios. Then a physio named Mary phoned up. I explained that I was sorry but the course was full. Later, after we had spoken (and laughed) on the phone for thirty minutes or more, I had not only allowed twenty-one on the course but I was also giving this girl a lift there! Mary became a special friend as she had an outsize sense of humour. We clicked. We went together to the evening course at Wendover to learn about Maitland's mobilisations and manipulations, and found infinitely more success using these techniques. We learned to move each of the joints of the spine with graduated force (grade 1–4) or, if necessary, click them (grade 5). Later, we attended a follow-up course and learned to move the other joints of the body (peripheral joints) to increase their range of movement and ease pain. This changed physiotherapy treatment FOREVER.

John told us that one of the highlights of his career had occurred the previous week. A young lady had attended for treatment with a painful lower back. She was asked to remove her roll-on and John left the cubicle. Ages afterwards, there was a muffled voice calling, 'HELP.' The patient's painful back had prevented her from peeling her corset downwards, so she had decided to remove it over her head and it had sprung back and she had become trapped with the rubber support circling her head and upward stretched arms rendering her helpless! Fortunately, they both had a hyperacute sense of the ridiculous.

I attended another course on the use of soundwaves (ultrasound) for assisting tissue healing but was appalled to hear that one patient with painful heel spurs had this new treatment with much too high a dosage and both the calcaneal bones of his heels collapsed. I never forgot this salutary lesson or the power of soundwaves.

At this time, I was concerned that the chairs in the physiotherapy waiting room were tatty, scruffy and decidedly inglorious. I asked the physiotherapy superintendent if we could have some new seats. She said that there was no point in asking, as the hospital had no money, so I asked her if she minded if I spoke to the hospital manager. She sighed, which I took to be an agreement. Without waiting further, I ran up three floors to the hospital manager's office and arrived completely out of breath. 'Come in, my dear,' he said. I huffed, puffed and huffed some more, until I eventually gasped that we needed some more welcoming chairs in the physiotherapy department, to which he replied, 'Of course, my dear.' It was as easy as that!

At about this time, I was delighted to discover that I was pregnant but not so happy with the accompanying nausea. I was given pills to combat the sickness I was experiencing at night, which I kept under the pillow, as I was not happy taking any medication while I was pregnant. Thank goodness I was cautious, as these tablets could easily have been thalidomide, which caused a serious failure of foetal limb development, one of the worst side effects of medication to unborn babies. I went for an antenatal check-up and found that my baby was intending to enter the world upside down and to confirm this, I was X-rayed with a ruler between my legs to make sure the head would fit through my pelvic outlet. The wonderful pre-natal scans were yet to be invented.

My husband had accepted a post in Canada, so I sold my sturdy Austin Cambridge to another physio for £40 (my brother still believes that I owe him £10), who used it as a chicken hutch! I wish I had kept the number plate FLY 408, as it would be worth decidedly more than the car even with the hens thrown in. Also, I am sure that the flightless chickens would not have appreciated having a hutch called FLY, but surely would have preferred an altogether much more apt name such as 'Chick Car', 'Auto-coop' or even 'Chicken Runabout' and given me their prestigious number plate!

When I was four months pregnant, I left West Herts and joined my husband in Burlington, south of Toronto, where we rented an apartment overlooking Lake Ontario. The road from Toronto Airport was banked on each side with a wall of snow six feet high, which had been thrown up merrily by the snow-clearing truck. It was bitterly cold. When I visited the doctor for a check-up and used a medical term, he found out that I was a physiotherapist, so persuaded me to work at the Joseph Brant Memorial Hospital in Burlington, where they were short-staffed. I travelled to the hospital by Greyhound bus, which, fortunately, ran exactly to time to prevent passengers freezing to death at the bus stops. As I increased in size (around, sadly not upwards), I enjoyed showing post-natal mothers how to perform pelvic floor exercises. It was fun. I worked three mornings a week and received the amount of a full-time physio in the UK. *Why work more?* I thought.

After two months, we came back home when Tony's contract expired prematurely, so I blew my hard-earned wages sightseeing for a day and a half in New York. The best part was taking a boat trip round Manhattan Island bounded by the Hudson, East and Harlem rivers, and seeing all the contrasting areas of New York from the water. Some were thriving, some were rundown needing rapid gentrification. I learned that the name Manhattan comes from the indigenous Munsi language, meaning island of many hills. It seemed to me that the good people of New York had taken this literally and created a city of man-made skyscraper mountains. The higher, the more imposing. People were everywhere, filling every sidewalk, people who seemed to know where they were going and were in a hurry to get there. All were beautifully dressed and stick thin, with, I noticed, perfectly aligned teeth. I was envious. Hundreds of yellow cabs streaked past, refusing to halt, delivering customers to diverse destinations. Eventually, we waited at a cab stop and found a willing cab driver, who drove us at the speed of a bullet to the airport without hitting anything on the way. Thus, reluctantly, we left the bustling metropolis and vowed to return in the future.

I was welcomed back at West Herts, where I created a senior post in the gym. I felt that I was ready for promotion to a more senior role with greater autonomy (and more money). Male patients in the men's leg group were asked to wear baggy navy-blue shorts which were provided by the hospital. They may have been too poor to own such luxuries! I quickly learned, firstly, that it was unwise to wear a dress and stand over the men lying on mats on the floor (the birth of up-skirting?), and secondly, to always face the men so that I could not see anything untoward dangling from their shorts. I gained permission to wear a tracksuit and thoroughly loved the independence of working in the gym.

The silliest thing that I ever did there was to remove the rubber ferrule from the bottom of the walking stick by standing on the handle and pulling strongly. Immediately, I felt pain in the middle of my thoracic spine, due to the pressure exerted when the ferrule suddenly popped off. One of my vertebrae collapsed and I lost a tweak more of my precious height. Sixty years later, I still feel pain in my upper back, mainly when washing up the saucepans!

My beautiful daughter, Claire, was born by breech presentation in August 1965, so after the short (six weeks') maternity leave, I volunteered to work Saturday mornings on the wards at West Herts, while my husband looked after our baby for three hours. It was wonderful to talk to adults and be appreciated by the inpatients. I also had a few domiciliary patients whom I treated in their homes. I used to treat one man while his wife was more than happy to look after Claire in her carrycot. I was one of the few mums who were able to work, so I paid a friend to look after Claire while I treated a few private patients. The only other young mother in our area who went to work was a doctor who lived close by, a fact which was accepted by the other young mothers, though there was definitely a stigma to working while caring for a baby in 1965.

The domiciliary patients that I treated were too frail to attend a physiotherapy department. I treated a lady with a severe stroke, giving her passive movements to her affected arm, helping her to balance and eventually to walk. It was a mammoth struggle. I could have done with another pair of hands (and a hoist). Another patient was bed-bound with multiple sclerosis, so I had to get her moving as best I could. Her uncaring teenage daughter objected to her mother paying for treatment, so she held on to her mother's purse and fired me. I felt for this brave patient, as it was bad enough having a ghastly progressive disease without having a bitch for a daughter. I treated one frail elderly lady who had such severe arthritis that she never left the house. She announced that she was allergic to all types of weather and kept the curtains tightly drawn. I had a key to let myself in and was always fearful that I would be the first person to find her dead in bed.

Sometimes there were special moments. I was invited to Ascot by one generous lady, to the royal enclosure, no less. The downside was that she wanted me to push her wheelchair across the hallowed lawn and she was heavy to shift. Sometimes physios have to take the rough with the smooth, though I was mortified to meet her grown-up son in our party, who absolutely refused to push his mother around or indeed help me. The next day, another patient invited me to Ascot, this time in a box, which was even better as I did not have to do any pushing or shoving.

I also treated a lovely overweight lady with arthritic knees, who became a friend, and when she sadly died, I went to her funeral. Her friends knew all about me, as she had related to them all the gossipy stories that I had brought to her from the outside world. Her family kindly invited me to a fortnight's holiday in Sandy Bay, Barbados, travelling, would you believe, by Concorde! There, I water-skied every afternoon and played tennis every evening with her grandchildren. Oh, the perks of private practice!

My wonderful son, Martin, arrived in November 1966, hitting the world headfirst, and after a slight pause, I continued working Saturday mornings and doing some private work. Then, serendipity, West Herts opened a staff crèche so I could return to West Herts for five mornings a week. Claire and Martin had the dubious honour of being the first two children in the crèche! In fact, they sat on the steps waiting for it to open. I was asked to be deputy physiotherapy superintendent at West Herts, but, although I liked the honour and the extra money would have helped, I declined the offer, as I was happy working just mornings, looking after my toddlers and seeing my private patients.

It was at this time that I learned that my husband was being unfaithful. This was such a gigantic shock and upset me emotionally. When I told him that I knew of his infidelity, he said that I was imagining it and that the 'men in the white coats' would come and take me away. I would cook a meal for 6.30pm and he would come home at 10pm or even later without having phoned me. There were no mobile phones then, but courtesy should have dictated that if you wanted to stay late you found a telephone to phone home. There was one in his office, for goodness' sake. I said to him, 'Even if you are with the Queen, she will think more of you rather than less of you, if you say that you must let your wife know that you will be late home.' It fell on deaf ears. There was no microwave oven then, so I produced what was called the 'three-ring dinner', where a meal would be heated over a saucepan of water and the gravy would shrink to reveal three rings. Tony's job as an export sales manager meant that he worked abroad for six weeks, then was home for six weeks, and even though the children and I had no contact for the six weeks while he was away, he always found a phone to ask me to pick him up from London Airport. I felt that I was being disrespected.

Chapter 5

Kodak Ltd

As my marriage began cracking at the seams, I became more ambitious and keen to pursue my career. In 1973, I learned that Kodak Ltd at Hemel Hempstead was looking for a physiotherapist and had approached the wife of a GP. I felt miffed that there was no advertisement and no level playing field, so, feeling emboldened and more than a little put out, I applied for the post. My interview consisted of being led into a smoke-filled room where the medical director and site doctor sat imposingly behind a large desk smoking their socks off. 'Would you like a cigarette?' one of them asked, to which I answered politely, 'No, thank you, I don't smoke,' trying desperately to hide my prejudice as best I could, as I wanted this job! I was appalled to see doctors, not just smoking, but smoking in the workplace. Passive smoking was unheard of then, but I must say that I felt most uncomfortable sitting in the room in this unhealthy fug. I looked through the mist and saw two doctors in dark suits, one good-looking and one not so.

The handsome one commenced the interview: 'Do you have children?'

'Yes, I have two school-age children,' I replied.

'What will happen in the holidays?' he enquired.

'My parents are retired teachers and will have then to stay in Dorset in the holidays,' I responded.

'This post is for three mornings a week and will gradually develop to include more hours [*it never did!*], would you be comfortable with that arrangement?' he asked.

'Yes, that is great,' I replied enthusiastically.

They asked me no questions about physiotherapy (whether I could rub the right way), which I thought was rather unusual, but I must have satisfied their requirements (they must have wanted a petite physio with a blonde ponytail – or perhaps they were desperate!) as they let me know there and then that I was successful. I left the smoky room, taking the smell with me, and was shown a large airy physiotherapy department with three cubicles divided by sympathetically designed, royal blue curtains and a modern office for me. I was walking on air until I drove out of the Kodak car park and my MGB GT became stuck on the exit road flaps. I had to ask the men on the gate to lower them before I could drive home, because my cherished car was so low on the road. For the next ten years, the men on the gate saw my classic car coming, waved and kindly lowered their lethal flaps for me.

I telephoned my parents to let them know the good news and gave them the dates of the forthcoming holidays. We arranged that I would take Claire and Martin as far as Stockbridge, meet my parents there and hand over my precious cargo. This arrangement worked extremely well for the next few years. Claire and Martin particularly liked being in the workshop with Grandpop, where they had stools to stand on so that they could reach the bench, while they hammered, chiselled and sawed with gusto. They each had their cherished toolboxes, which they still have to this day.

I handed in my notice to the superintendent physiotherapist at West Herts, who was rather shocked that I had not asked her for a reference. In fact, she was extremely curt and unsympathetic in my wish to advance my career. Eventually, after patiently listening to her diatribe for a tad too long, as I was leaving her room I turned and asked her, 'Can't you just SAY that you are sorry that I am leaving?' She failed to respond. I returned to the gym in tears. The patients there couldn't understand why I was unhappy when I was going on to a more prestigious post. THEY congratulated me warmly. My patients were lovely.

I loved my time at Kodak. I loved working on my own without a cold superintendent watching my every move. The physiotherapy room became a relaxed and welcoming place for workers to enter, and I was free at last to develop my own personality and have a laugh with the patients under my care.

I have many memories of my time at Kodak. I shall never forget a friendly man who was referred for treatment to his shoulder. As I chatted to him, he unbuttoned his shirt and I was horrified to see his right arm come off too. I had to leave the cubicle to compose myself. The referral failed to mention that he was an amputee.

Another time, I was teaching a man to do breathing exercises while he was standing up. As he breathed in and out, his trousers started to descend. I was mesmerised, mainly because he was prepared to let them descend slowly to his ankles without pulling them back up. I must admit that I had to stifle my mirth until I left the room before laughing uncontrollably. Each time I started to walk back into the room, the giggles erupted, until eventually I managed to control myself in a more professional manner. 'What shall I do now?' he said, to which I replied, 'How about putting your braces on and starting again?'

On another occasion, the doctor entered the treatment room and asked to speak to me. I said that I was unable to come out of the cubicle as a patient was sitting on my dress. Swift as a spitting cobra, he entered the cubicle to find that a portly gentleman with paralysed muscles from polio had transferred (with my inept help) from his wheelchair onto the plinth and had landed on my dress.

I enjoyed my time at Kodak immensely. I was expected to treat two patients at a time by popping one on traction while I treated another with ultrasound, or giving one patient shortwave diathermy while teaching exercises to another. Kodak benefitted, as it saved the staff from having a morning off work to attend the local hospital. As an occupational physiotherapist, I could also advise whether the employees' workstation should be modified to prevent injuries such as back pain or repetitive strain injury.

In 1969, we moved to Chesham Bois from Chesham for two reasons. Firstly, a little boy had cycled down the hill and was tragically killed by a lorry on the main road, and secondly, our paedophile neighbour was due out of prison after molesting a girl of four years of age. Claire was then aged four and Martin aged three when we moved out of the area. While the removal men were lugging the furniture into the new family home, my neighbour, Margot, came across to me and asked if I was a physio from The London. What were my chances of living next door to another physio? I asked her if she recognised me, but she replied that I kept saying, 'Jolly good,' which was an expression we used to praise and encourage our patients when they had exercised correctly. I vowed there and then to eliminate 'Jolly Good' from my vocabulary.

I settled into our lovely new house thinking how lucky I was to be living in such a pleasant area, when out of the blue I received a telephone call from a sixteen-year-old girl who was in floods of tears. Apparently, my husband (aged thirty) had made her pregnant and she wanted to get in touch with him. I calmed her down and offered to meet her and give her money for an abortion, which she tearfully refused. The next day, she phoned again to say that she had had an abortion. I never believed that this could happen in such a short time frame and believed that Tony was standing over her and making her make that call.

Life carried on. The children needed a father. Divorce was not an option. Tony had a vicious temper and would push me about. One time I ran away from him and locked the bedroom door and jumped into bed. He pushed his shoulder against the door and splintered the door frame before gathering up the duvet and throwing it down the stairs, leaving me in the foetal position, trembling. After these rants he would eventually calm down and life would go on. I confided in my girlfriends, who helped me emotionally, but sadly, I was unable to open up to my mother, even though she was a voluntary marriage guidance counsellor.

Much later, I was invited to the leaving celebration of one of the directors at Kodak. Initially, I declined attending as I was nursing my mother at home with terminal cancer. When he said that it was important to him, as I was the one person who had enabled him to walk again, I asked a kind friend to sit with my mother for a few hours, so he was able to thank me in his leaving speech. What a thoughtful and generous man.

My mother was so bound up with life at Union Church in Totteridge that I thought she was mad to want to retire to Dorset. I was wrong. My parents quickly entered into village life centred around the church and the village hall. When I visited, I was introduced to their elderly friends as 'Grace, the physiotherapist', before being regaled with everyone's aches and pains; everything from housemaid's knee to ingrown toenails, I seem to remember. This was always tricky to cope with, as firstly, it is impossible to give the correct advice without a full assessment, and secondly, I was trying and failing to have a break from work. My parents were happily content in their new garden: Mother tended the flowers and Pop produced vegetables all year round (plus a goodly amount for the wild rabbits which arrived regularly from the surrounding countryside). Mother never lost her authority as, in the days before the mobile phone, she used to 'command' Pop to come in from the large garden for meals by ringing a large school bell.

I nursed my mother for three weeks until she was too ill for me to cope and needed terminal care in hospital. She was taken to hospital, where she died peacefully from liver cancer. She was just seventy. Her life had been fulfilled; she had run a brilliant nursery school, had been a church deacon, she had borne three children and had six beloved grandchildren. She was a wonderful grandmother. I thought at the time that she had been fortunate to have lived for 'three score years and ten' but now that I am older than that myself, I believe that she was robbed from enjoying further happy years by her cruel cancer.

I built up a private practice at my new home. I booked the first two appointments to run consecutively so that the patients would think I was running a busy practice. I made sure that I was always home when the children came home from school. The room directly to the left of the front door became my treatment room, and if the door was closed the children knew not to enter. Martin used to pop notes for me under the door, and one time he even slid his school report under before running away! Claire told her father that she thought I wasn't working as she could hear laughter coming through the door.

I bought an ultrasound machine and used it for a man from the squash club who was suffering with tennis elbow. He was the only patient who refused to pay me so, after repeated requests over a number of weeks, I settled myself in his office until he paid my bill. I had heard a story of one man who was owed money, who sat in his debtor's office with a smelly wet fish in his pocket. Fortunately, I did not have to resort to such tactics!

My accountant advised me to run an expensive car as a way of offsetting my tax, so I took him at his word and bought a beautiful brand-new red Porsche 924, which was a joy to drive for a number of glorious years until the head gasket leaked and the engine BLEW UP. It was a sad day; I loved that car more than any other before or since. The manufacturers were not sympathetic to a poor physio with a Porsche and refused to repair it as it was out of warranty. As the maintenance costs were way out of pocket for a humble physiotherapist, and reluctantly after doing the sums, I had to sell it. I sold it to a garage in Bushey and one day, I was walking across a zebra crossing in the village when my cherished red car failed to stop for me and I was nearly mown down in my prime by my pride and joy.

One businessman came to see me and requested massage for his aching back. As I started to massage him, his breathing changed and he went, not so soundly, to sleep on my new couch. This left me in a predicament: should I stop rubbing him or should I wake him up? In the end I practised all my noisy percussion techniques, such as hacking with the sides of my hand and clapping with cupped hands until he woke blearily, felt better and paid the bill.

I bought a portable faradic battery and tested it on my son, Martin. He was intrigued and asked me if he could take it to school! Thank goodness he had asked me. The thought of a schoolboy giving electric shocks to his friends (or foes) was too ghastly to contemplate. Can you just imagine the conversation I would have had with his headmaster?

I treated a child who had flat feet with faradism and exercises. As his mother did not believe he had flat feet, I painted his soles and stood him on a piece of paper to demonstrate the lack of medial and anterior arches. To show this unconvinced mother what the arches of a normal foot looked like, I called Martin into the room and tickled his soles with paint. Oh dear… That was when I realised that my son also had flat feet!

I loved my children, but my marriage was falling apart. Tony was tall (six feet, three inches), dark and handsome, but sadly suffered from a violent temper. I tried to cope with the physical and mental abuse as best I could. When he erupted, I felt like leaving through the cat flap. I took to locking the bathroom door when I was having a bath so my husband could not make unkind comments about my body (and that was when I was a size twelve!). When we returned from seeing friends, there would always be a post-mortem and Tony would make comments such as, 'What did you say that for?' or, 'Your laugh is dreadful,' and even, 'Don't stand next to her, she is really pretty.' I felt belittled. Today, it would be called bullying. I confided in my school friend Jenny, Dorothy from Harrow, Mary from Amersham and Judy from West Herts. They were wonderful and listened sympathetically as I poured out my heart to them. Talking to my friends, particularly those with an outsize sense of humour, helped to put everything into perspective, so I knew that it was not me who was being unreasonable. Much, much later, when I had my seventieth birthday, I invited ten close girlfriends to a dinner party and to stay the night in a hotel with a swimming pool as a thank you for their wonderfully warm friendship and stalwart support.

The punishment at home seemed to escalate. When we returned from one party, I told Tony off for fondling a friend's large boobs. Immediately, he leaped up from his chair with a thunderous glare and pinned me against the wall with his hands round my throat. I froze. I was scared rigid. He was so large that if I had fought him, I would have lost. I was prepared to die. Suddenly he said, 'No, I can't do it, I love you too much.' For my sanity and my welfare, I knew the marriage could not survive.

At this time, for my recreation I enjoyed playing tennis and squash, and regularly found a childminder so that I could play home and away tennis and squash matches. I was happiest among a circle of good friends at dinner parties and dances. I lived for Saturday nights. We always went abroad on holiday with other families. We were the Happy Doreys! I wanted family life for the children, but at what expense? Very few couples split up in those days, as there was still a stigma surrounding the word 'divorce'. I did not have the guts to separate until I heard that my friend Judy was divorcing her husband and I thought, *If she can do it, so can I.*

I went to see a solicitor, who was recommended by a friend, and she agreed that I had more than enough grounds for a divorce (probably for a number of divorces!). She commented, 'I can't understand you. Most girls come in here and bawl their eyes out, and you are completely dry-eyed.'

I told her, 'This is such a relief after twenty years of living with a husband with an uncontrollable temper, who delights in taking it out on me.' I left her room and was totally unable to see the steps down from her office to the pavement as I was engulfed in tears, not just a bit of snivelling needing gentle dabbing, but heart-wrenching sobbing needing a couple of boxes of man-sized tissues. I had to wait until the flood had finally abated before I was able to drive home.

Then, I had the impossible task of telling Tony. I arranged to tell him at 11am on a Saturday morning when the children would be at home, as he never pushed me around when they were there. The kitchen was in the front of the house, so I removed all the knives, turned on the lights and opened the outside door to the road. I alerted a neighbour, as I was expecting trouble. I waited until Tony was in the kitchen and, as I readied myself for a quick exit, I said, 'I have been to see a solicitor and I want a divorce.'

He replied, 'You're very brave,' and crumpled onto a stool and wept. The end of the road. There was no going back. I felt like the worm who had turned. So sadly, when Claire was seventeen and Martin was sixteen, with newfound courage, I divorced my husband after twenty years of marriage and replaced him with a tool to open the marmalade.

It is a credit to both children that they passed their A-levels and O-levels while suffering the trauma of their parents' separation, especially as at school they were then among a minority of children from split homes. I was very proud of them. Still am. Claire went on to Goldsmiths College to study art and is a talented artist. Martin went to Manchester University to study film and is now a successful author.

I spoke to a friend who owned an insurance company and found that I would be able to afford to stay in the house and take over the mortgage. To fund my outrageously expensive divorce (and buy my lawyer a tropical island), I sold some land adjoining the house to my neighbour, provided that he erected a six-foot-high fence between our properties. 'I will put up a five-foot-high fence, as you will not be able to see over that,' he contemptuously commented. You can imagine how I replied to this height-related put down! The sale was only 'on' if he adhered to my stipulations. He sheepishly agreed. After which, he wrote a letter to Tony to say that he could understand why he wanted a divorce!

I needed to work full-time to be able to keep a roof over our heads, so after ten years at Kodak, I started to look for a physiotherapy manager's post.

Chapter 6

BUPA Hospital Bushey

I applied to BUPA Hospital Bushey, a newly built private hospital, to be the physiotherapy superintendent, and was interviewed by a rheumatology consultant and the hospital manager. The consultant had his own agenda and asked, 'What do you think of hydrotherapy?'

'It is brilliant,' I replied. 'The patients find it so beneficial.'

I saw the rheumatologist smile to the manager as much to say, 'I told you that we needed a pool here for my private patients.'

That evening, I was telephoned by the hospital manager's secretary, who DID NOT say, 'Mrs Dorey, we are pleased to let you know that you were successful in your application for the post of physiotherapy superintendent.' She just said abruptly, 'You've got the job!'

I handed in my notice to Kodak, and the staff and a few patients took me out for a delicious lunch to celebrate my new role at BUPA and thank me for being their physio for ten years.

Unbeknown to me, there was a hiccup, as the speeches were hastily rescheduled until the end of the luncheon. Apparently, one of my patients (the guy with polio who had sat on my dress) had drawn a brilliant cartoon of me having lumbar traction being suspended only by my fingertips and toes. The framed cartoon had fallen off the easel and the glass had shattered, so one of the workers was sent hastily to the glaziers to fix another piece of glass. I was honoured to receive this thoughtful gift, together with a carriage clock and an armful of flowers. I was embarrassed as I thought that I should have been thanking THEM for making my life so enjoyable for ten years. I look back on my time at Kodak with affection, as it was a privilege to be their physio.

At BUPA, I promptly changed my job title to physiotherapy manager because it sounded more impressive and started full-time work in January 1983, the same day that my husband left home for good and went to live with Pat, a beautiful estate agent. Six months later, they were married in Amersham. Cruelly, Claire and Martin were not invited to their wedding. The happy couple moved away and regularly I had to ask Tony to come and visit his children. I was saddened that they never had the children for Christmas or took them on holiday. Eventually, Tony suffered from prostate cancer and endured ten years of intensive treatment until tragically he died. Claire and Martin wanted me to come with them to his funeral in Ipswich, where I was reacquainted with a few of his school friends. It was a sad day, saying goodbye to my teenage sweetheart and grieving for the marriage that might have been. However, the day was made much, much worse when I discovered that he had not left a legacy for his children.

To make ends meet, I still saw my private patients in the evening and at weekends. To add insult to injury, I had to work a Saturday morning and be on call for the hospital EVERY

OTHER weekend as there was only one other member of staff. I had a bleep, and when it went off my heart would sink and I had to find a telephone (no mobiles then) and ring the hospital, sometimes just to find that the nurses only wanted a walking stick or an ice pack on someone's knee! You can imagine what I said to them. However, I never minded if it was a serious request for post-operative breathing, huffing, coughing, or postural drainage for a congested or collapsed lung, as I was pleased to be able to help. It was a privilege to be able to improve the lives of my patients. I loved the career that I had chosen. Most patients improved and the majority were unfailingly grateful.

In 1977, the Department of Health established autonomy for physiotherapists and our days of being the doctor's handmaidens were gone for ever. Thank goodness. No longer could the medical profession be prescriptive. We were at last able to assess and diagnose before giving the relevant treatment and advice to our patients. We expected referrals to come from the consultants or GPs saying only, 'Physiotherapy please.'

Gradually as the workload increased, I recruited more staff until we had twenty full-time or part-time physios. There was a wonderful welcoming atmosphere in the department. All of us made sure that our patients enjoyed their visits. I felt that coming to work should be a pleasure for the staff, not like the days that I dreaded appearing at the dreary physical treatment centre in Harrow. We shared news, gossip and humour. I was always delighted when one of the staff announced that they were pregnant. Although, one member of staff who was not married came to me in tears and sadly announced that she was pregnant and that she could not possibly tell her mother. 'Mothers are lovely people,' I told her. 'I am sure that she will be supportive. I expect that she will be delighted to be a granny.' The next day my valued member of staff came to me to tell me that, indeed, her mother was thrilled.

The physios were a tightly knit group, a happy bunch, but if anyone from another part of the hospital dared to say anything untoward about the physios, we stuck together in united defiance. Many of the staff became firm friends with each other and I loved being with my younger colleagues. I was caught up in their excitement when they were making wedding preparations, thrilled when they gave birth and pleased to hear about their family events. I became a sort of 'mother hen', giving heartfelt support when they suffered a bereavement or empathising if their marriage was in difficulty. Physios struggled in to work even when they were ill, so if they wore a cardigan and looked shivery, I sent them home, even if they protested that they were letting their patients down. I told them, 'It is much better to stay home and keep warm than spread the infection to everybody else.' The rest of the staff always coped with the extra workload. There were now enough staff to cover weekend duties, so they organised the weekend rota and on-call duties among themselves, which took a load of pressure off me.

The female staff wore a white dress with a navy-blue belt; the male staff wore a white tunic top over navy trousers, though sometimes their tops were not so white! I sent one Australian physio to the laundry department to be ironed as he looked as if he had slept in his uniform (perhaps he had!) and he came back grinning, having had his tunic washed, dried and ironed by the pretty young girl working there. We were meant to wash our own uniform, so his charm had beaten the system. One girl from Australia used Sellotape to keep the hem of her dress up for far too many weeks, until I found a needle and cotton and hemmed her dress up for her. I even wrote a letter to her mother in Australia to say that I was looking after her! I wanted the staff to look smart. I was turning into Miss Orme!

As the work expanded, we moved the site of the department four times within the hospital to gain larger and larger rooms.

At last, I worked with beds that moved up and down electrically, which was a godsend, so the hideous wooden massage platforms were never needed. We had all the necessary equipment to be able to treat patients effectively. Fortunately, the majority of patients had medical insurance. We provided a high standard of care, treating our patients individually and giving them our undivided time. Inpatients were given treatment six days a week. Most treatment was effective and we discharged our outpatients when they were at least eighty per cent better, knowing that they would continue to improve if they adhered to the correct advice. We believed that the majority of orthopaedic pain could be alleviated by physical means, but if patients failed to improve, we either sent them back to their GP for further tests or we referred them on to the most suitable specialist.

In the physiotherapy department, we used to sit with our patients while they were receiving passive treatment, such as shortwave, wax treatment to soothe hands or feet (provided we had remembered to switch the wax bath on to melt the wax), or on traction. When I sat with one female patient who was strapped around her chest and pelvis on the traction apparatus to stretch her back gently and relieve her lower back pain, she asked me if I was married. 'I am divorced,' I whispered quietly, to which she answered in a voice that could have cut through concrete, 'Oh, I do not know anyone who is divorced. All my family and friends are happily married.' Physiotherapists have feelings. I had to control my emotions, be professional and suppress the desire to wind the handle up even further! (I could have made her ten feet tall!)

When the traction machine broke down, the physios panicked. I was able to fix a rope to the lower harness and, using a pulley system, I added weights to the rope to produce the required amount of traction. This was how we gave traction in the old days! I would like to think that the physios were impressed, but it was more likely that I showed them that I was from an extinct generation!

As I was on my own, I started to look for possible holidays that were out of the ordinary. I noticed in the *Physiotherapy Journal* that there was a Physiotherapy Study Tour of Russia run by The Chartered Society of Physiotherapy, so I contacted my physio friends, Dorothy and Judy, and we agreed to go together. We were interested to see Russia as it emerged from the Cold War. During the 1980s, Perestroika called for reform of the Communist Union and glasnost, meaning 'openness', allowed visits from foreigners provided they were accompanied by a Russian official. We welcomed this insight into another culture. We visited hospitals and clinics in Moscow and Leningrad, and were saddened to see some of the antique physiotherapy equipment that they used, while newly donated equipment lay unused in the corridors. In Moscow, we visited the Red Square, the Kremlin, St Basil's Cathedral and Lenin's tomb, where we were pushed into file rather roughly by large Russian guards wearing imposing grey sheepskin uniform. Lenin's body had been preserved and looked almost transparent. No wonder he looked so frail; he had died in 1924, so had been embalmed for sixty-four years.

I am sure we can admit after this length of time, that it was Judy who plugged her hairdryer into the socket in our bedroom in Leningrad and fused the power in the whole hotel! We cleaned the carbon flash from the socket and pretended that we were not culpable. The innocent English! How could we defend ourselves when the only Russian word we could think of was '*Kaput*' (and that was a German word borrowed by the Soviets).

The highlight for me was seeing the magnificent Kirov Ballet, which included a performance from their highly skilled young dancers, the stars of the future. Each ballet was blissfully sublime. I was in heaven. We had queued for seats not required by Russian dignitaries and for a few roubles we found ourselves being directed to blue velvet armchairs in the front row of this amazingly sculpted theatre. In fact, after each ballet we started a standing ovation on our side of the theatre by rising to our feet and clapping vigorously! We also visited the Hermitage and saw the amazing Cinderella staircase; the exquisite, priceless Amber Room; and the fabulous interior décor, displaying the largest collection of paintings in the world. An unforgettable experience.

When we were leaving Leningrad Airport, as we went through security, one of the officials found a can of hair lacquer in Judy's carry-on bag. He spoke no English but took us into a small room, where Judy insisted that I accompanied her, then he sprayed a jet and lit it to demonstrate how dangerous hairspray could be. There was a spurt of orange/yellow flame similar to a jet engine, causing us to tremble in terror. He confiscated the can and fortunately let us through, but it was rather an unnerving experience and so difficult when you don't speak the language.

The following year there was a Physiotherapy Study Tour of China, which Judy, her new hairdryer and I decided to join. The previous year, 1989, was marked by the ghastly massacre of hundreds of students who were peacefully demonstrating in favour of modernisation and democracy in Tiananmen Square, so The Chartered Society of Physiotherapy had decided not to endorse this trip. As I had previously toured Russia, I was telephoned by the tour company to know if I would like to be the leader on this trip. FREE. Would I? So, the cost of the whole trip was refunded. What a welcome bonus! We visited hospitals and clinics under the close direction of a Chinese guide and saw the diverse level of physiotherapy in this amazing country. Also, we were taken to a junior school where we were entertained by a delightful performance of singing from the most beautiful children in the world. In the hospitals, we were saddened to see children with harelips and those with club feet in wheelchairs, who had been abandoned by their parents so that they were allowed to have a normal baby under the one-child policy. In the West, these little children would have been given surgery and a chance of a normal life. We saw many cots containing babies with facial deformities, who were tightly swaddled and fed whilst lying down. It was heart-breaking.

We went to Beijing and were amazed at the vast size of Tiananmen Square, one of the largest city squares in the world, where we saw bullet holes, the evidence of the previous year's massacre. We visited the Forbidden City in all its impressive glory. We were taken to the magnificent Great Wall, where I climbed its steep steps with difficulty, while the taller girls leaped ahead like nimble gazelles. I bet the horses who used to patrol the wall in former times made a better job of it! At Xian, in a hanger the size of a football pitch, we saw rows of life-sized Terracotta soldiers, each individually sculpted, a breathtaking experience, one of the most amazing attractions in the world, for which I felt they could have trebled or even quadrupled the entrance fee to visitors from abroad as the admission charges were so ridiculously cheap. It was amazing to think what these guards protecting the afterlife of Qin Shi Huang, the first Emperor of China, must have looked like almost two thousand years ago when they were painted in an array of bright colours. In Guilin, we saw cormorants fishing in the beautiful Li River, which is surrounded by exquisitely shaped limestone crags, which have been captured for posterity by many Chinese artists. I felt it was cruel that the cormorants had elastic bands tied round their throats, so that they were unable to swallow the fish that they had kindly caught for their owner.

We finished our tour in Hong Kong, with its bustling population under garish, bright lights, a far cry from Mainland China. It was a culture shock. We had all lost weight on this trip. Chinese food was not like it is in the UK. They started with the pudding, which usually consisted of dates with rice; then they served a main course of chicken, with EVERY part of it, including its feet and beak, chopped up with vegetables; then to finish we were given a thin soup to fill the empty spaces! We missed potatoes as, in China, these were given to the pigs. Having lived on a diet of rice for two weeks, the first thing that we did when we arrived in Hong Kong was to find a McDonald's and order some chips!

The next year, undaunted, I approached the tour company myself and volunteered to lead a Multidisciplinary Study Tour of China – FREE, of course (to all the places that I had read about and wanted to visit). They readily agreed. We viewed the medical care in Shanghai, Lhasa, Chengdu, Chongqing and Wuhan in the company of a delightful Chinese guide. Included in the trip was a cruise down the mighty Yangtze River viewing the magnificent scenery of the three gorges before they were flooded when the dam was completed downstream, providing the largest water conservation project in the world. The Yangtze was fast-flowing and we were appalled to see a bloated dead body floating past. The tributaries were coloured a clear turquoise and there was a definite demarcation where they flowed into the main muddy-brown river (the longest river in Asia and the third longest in the world). We were very aware that when the dam was completed and the river level rose, many of the homes on the banks would be underwater. In fact, in the seventeen years it took to complete the Three Gorges Dam, China relocated a million people.

Sadly, many of us had altitude sickness when we flew into Llasa, the capital of Tibet, at an altitude of almost twelve thousand feet, suffering from a severe headache at the base of the skull, tingling fingers and toes, an increased heart rate and difficulty breathing. Fortunately, we had a doctor in our multidisciplinary team and, despite the severe symptoms and with his kind administrations, we all survived. Three days later when we had just about acclimatised, we were able to visit the Potala Palace (with its many staircases), which was the home of the Dalai Lama until 1959, and which is now a World Heritage site. It was absolutely breathtakingly amazing. The highlight of the tour.

I returned from such a fascinating holiday (sorry, study tour) rather reluctantly, so when a young lad arrived in a hat for treatment, I nit-picked: 'Would you like to take your hat off now you are inside?' He did but, being a good Jewish boy, he had another hat on underneath.

We used to have orthodox female Jewish patients who wore wigs, and I found it was difficult to manipulate their necks and keep their wigs on straight. Only one lady bravely volunteered to take her wig off. I never felt that I could ask these ladies to remove their headgear.

Once, I followed a tall lady into the treatment room and was surprised that she was wearing a grey wig. I thought to myself, *If I wore a wig, I would have a blonde one.* She handed me her referral which read, 'This transgender patient is transitioning from male to female. Please could she have pelvic floor exercises to prevent her spraying urine once her penis is removed.' I deliberated whether I should use the male continence assessment form or the female continence assessment form, and decided to use the female version but calmly crossed out the diagram of the vagina. She asked me if I would talk to the local transgender club where she was active, but I politely refused this invitation as I felt decidedly out of my depth. On further consideration, I believe I should have gone and listened, so that I could have understood the thoughts and feelings of these brave people.

It is extraordinary that one remembers the calamities at work more than the successes. We had one physio who was known for her clumsiness. If there was a crash in the department, I would instantly call out her name! One day, she excelled herself and spilled hot wax over a patient's jacket. I was free at that time, so while I seethed quietly to myself, I picked off the solidified wax until his tweed was wax-free. Phew!

As physiotherapy manager, I was ultimately responsible for any problems. One of the physios treated a charming lady who, unfortunately, sustained an ice burn to her knee even though the ice had been placed over a damp cloth for just ten minutes. It was a very unpleasant burn, much worse than a thermal burn or scald. Apparently, when the patient was quizzed about her past history, she reported that she had previously had a thrombosis in that leg, which must have compromised the circulation of her blood. We saw her daily and dressed her knee until it healed, and we both breathed a sigh of relief.

Sometimes the unexpected happens. I was treating a lad of seventeen years of age for his back and neck problems. He stripped down to his pants and lay face down on the sheet I had placed on the bed with his nose through the face hole. His buttocks and legs were covered with a blanket. I pressed on each of his cervical, thoracic and lumbar spines to find out which joints caused his pain. Suddenly he leaped up, saying, 'Sorry, sorry.' He had ejaculated onto the sheet. To spare his embarrassment, I scooped up the sheet and said, 'Don't worry, this happens all the time,' as I gave him some tissues and left the room. He did not book an appointment for further treatment.

Years later, I was walking down the corridor of the hospital and a confident man approached me. 'You do not know who I am,' he announced.

'No, I am sorry,' I said.

'I am the man who came over your bed,' he said, whereupon I kindly replied, 'I am sorry, I do not remember.'

Interestingly, if I met former patients outside the hospital, I would recognise their faces but would always struggle to remember their names. It was an annoying type of word blindness, though I could always remember the part of the body that I had treated, so I could always have a meaningful conversation by asking questions such as, 'How is your knee now? Were you able to run the marathon?' I must have treated thousands and thousands of patients, so it was no surprise to me that more often than not my memory let me down.

I went on a Health and Safety course once and was astounded when the lecturer asked twenty of us to give our names and then repeated everyone's names back correctly. What a gift. We deliberately changed places and asked her to name us again. She was word perfect. I would have needed the delegates to wear large name badges.

When I worked at Kodak, patient notes included a passport-sized photograph of the patient, so I would instantly know who was coming for treatment. This was a godsend for someone like me. Looking back, I should have introduced this system to BUPA (provided I gained patient consent).

Once, I treated a lady who I will never forget, though her name escapes me. I treated her ankle injury with ultrasound and then placed a stirrup of Elastoplast around her lower leg to prevent her ankle turning inwards. When she returned for treatment, I removed it, and, to my horror, a full thickness of skin under her heel came away with the plaster. I was mortified. I quickly replaced the plaster (and skin) and asked her to attend the department every day for the next week without charge. Luckily nature was kind to us both and the skin adhered back on to her heel. I breathed a sigh of relief. Now, we place thin gauze next to the skin before applying sticky plaster.

Most of our patients needed treatment for their painful necks or backs, so treatment became predictably routine. It was our bread and butter. Occasionally, we would be reminded that all patients were individuals who suffered stress in differing ways. I was gaily massaging a lady's neck as her muscles were completely knotted up with spasm, when she started weeping. 'No-one has touched me since my husband died.' How achingly sad, but a timely reminder of the power of touch.

Patients used to open up and unload when they were massaged. Detective inspectors would be wise to use this method to get criminals to own up and disclose the truth. Threatening the accused would only make them tighten up, but in a relaxed atmosphere they would be more likely to be candidly honest.

One day, a lady walked in and said without embarrassment, 'I am a hypochondriac. I have severe back pain. Can you help me?' I replied that I could help and that I would treat her myself. She was a good-natured patient who benefitted by some mobilisation to her lumbar spine coupled with a large helping of 'tender loving care'. I gave her buckets of reassurance to allay her anxiety and some home exercises to concentrate on when she was suffering discomfort. If only all people were so candid, so self-aware; it would make therapy so much easier. I thanked her for being so frank.

One morning, one of the part-time physios was brutally honest. She telephoned and left a message to say that she had been asked to treat a famous film star privately, so she would not be in for her shift. As she had abandoned a list of patients, I considered that she was a totally expendable member of staff. How could she desert her patients? I never employed her again.

The department became busier and busier, so I asked Hospital Manager (2) (hospital managers left regularly to be promoted to area managers and then directors) if we could have a dedicated physiotherapy department. I justified this by showing that we were at full capacity and even had a waiting list. I designed a new department to include four treatment rooms (instead of curtained cubicles) so that patients had audio as well as visual privacy. The new department included a large gym, an ultraviolet room and a splendid deck-level hydrotherapy pool with its own hoist.

When this was eventually built, each of the full-time staff bagged a room of their own, so if anyone was running late, they would only inconvenience themselves. This worked extremely well and gave the staff a sense of ownership, which in turn boosted their job satisfaction.

We had a formal opening of the department by Brian Hawkins, the head of BUPA Hospitals. Hospital Manager (3) had encouraged the new department and was very proud of our achievement. It was the first time that I had given a speech. I started by saying that I had rehearsed my speech in front of Oscar, my white Persian cat, who swiftly moved to another room, so if anyone felt so obliged, they were very welcome to explore the rest of the department. It was a wonderful opportunity to thank each member of staff who had contributed to our success. I mentioned that we had ordered some snazzy swimming trunks for Brian but, unfortunately, they had failed to arrive in time. 'They were embroidered with BUPA,' I said, 'as BUPA stands for Brian Undressed, Photography Allowed!' I then led the star visitor to the pool room and had a publicity photograph taken where I pretended to lower him into the pool fully dressed. What an opportunity!

I loved working in the warm pool using the buoyancy to assist patients' movement and the resistance of the water to build up their muscle strength. Unfortunately, because I was so small, I developed a headache at the top of my head when I was in the pool with a patient, so reluctantly I left the pool work to the taller staff who could work with their shoulders out of the water. Miss Orme would have drowned.

Once, a male physio walked round the edges of the pool, while his patient was moving table tennis bats up and down to exercise his shoulders, when the physio slipped into the

Claire and Martin as
toddlers

Claire at school

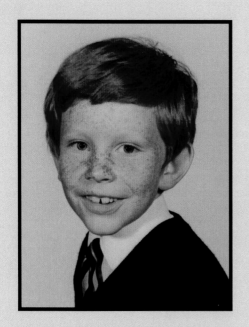

Martin at school

Mischa, my Golden Retriever

In the new gym at
BUPA Hospital Bushey

The opening of the new physiotherapy department
at BUPA Hospital Bushey

Brian Hawkins, the head of BUPA Hospitals, about to get his feet wet

Physiotherapists preparing for a study tour of China

Fiftieth Anniversary of the 1959
London Hospital School of physiotherapy set
From left to right: Polly, Rosie, Pat, Rocca, Jane,
Grace, Angela, Gill and Jeanine

Maggie being treated for leukaemia

*Grace receiving a MSc at the Barbican
photograph by Ede and Ravenscroft*

*Grace receiving a PhD at Bristol
Cathedral photograph by Ede and
Ravenscroft*

Jo, Martin, Grace and Claire at Buckingham Palace
photograph by Charles Green

Charlie and Maggie

Nick and Grace photograph by Karl Grimwade

water. The amazing thing was that the patient was absolutely unperturbed by the almighty splash, which completely covered the walls and part of the ceiling, and as it dripped down onto his head, he continued to move the bats up and down as if his life depended on it, while his patient notes floated away!

The pool was particularly good for hips and knees after joint replacement surgery. Patients came down from the wards in wheelchairs with waterproof dressings over their wounds and were lowered gently by hoist into the pool. They loved it. The buoyancy of the water supported their limbs while they cautiously exercised their new joints. However, one time, during the Great Storm of 1987, a large tree fell down across the road directly outside the hospital and missed a female patient's car by inches, so she arrived in the department terrified, trembling and white as a ghost with shock. I popped her in the warm pool and kept talking to her until her colour returned.

The maintenance men tested the pool acid/alkali balance daily and added chlorine as necessary. There were times after a bank holiday when, unhappily, the water turned a ghastly shade of green and the patients were not able to have pool therapy until it was crystal clear again. I received more complaints from patients about this problem than at any other time.

I employed a wonderful physiotherapy assistant named June, who would help patients not only get ready for pool therapy and get dressed afterwards, but also tidy the department and help on the wards as necessary. She was an angel and by far the most popular member of staff. We also had young girls visit to do work experience, as long as they were serious about a career in physiotherapy. I would always ask my patients if they minded the work experience girls sitting in on their treatment. Everyone was willing to help, except one lady, who refused point blank and, believe it or not, she was a teacher. One of these girls who helped us in the summer holidays desperately wanted to be a physio, so, as she was bright and had natural empathy with the patients, I rung up the principal of a training school whom I knew to pass on my recommendation and she was accepted. Then, I employed her as a helper when she was on holiday from university. When she qualified, I employed her. All the staff were more than willing to help her and one member of staff kindly became her mentor.

Once a week after work, I met three good friends, Ann, Mary and Liz, who worked in different departments within the hospital, at the local pub for supper. It was good to be able to unwind, be totally uninhibited and laugh, often uproariously, together. These evenings became increasingly important as the work increased in intensity. It was a great way of hearing in an informal way about life (and all the licentious gossip) in the rest of the hospital.

BUPA made the forward-thinking decision to computerise our appointment system to provide an electronic diary. All went well until there was a computer system failure and we had no idea who was coming in for treatment. We were unable to get the patient's notes out in advance and then totally unable to book further appointments. It was even worse for the consultants in outpatients, as they had to bring their patients' notes in from home. After this debacle we printed out the appointments for the next day and blew the paperless system.

We had a splendid receptionist named Sue, who made sure that patients were booked for the correct physio in the right room. Patients for UVL or traction needed to be booked separately to avoid doubling up. We noticed when other receptionists, however good-natured, made mistakes, that the department ran less smoothly, so that physios and patients had to wait for the correct room. This caused unnecessary frustration. One day, I interviewed a prospective receptionist who, I noticed, had the longest nails I had seen, so I asked her, 'Would you consider cutting your nails so that you look more professional?'

'Yes,' she replied, but when she arrived for work sporting long red talons, I mentioned that I had asked her to trim her nails. 'You asked me if I would consider it and I have considered it and I am not complying.' A little boy who accompanied his mother, who was having treatment, put it more succinctly when he commented in a shrill voice which pierced right through the department, 'Look at that lady's horrid nails.' Miss Orme would have been horrified.

I was sitting at the reception desk one day when a patient proudly wheeled a pram in containing her new baby. The patients and staff there made a big fuss of the baby boy and ignored his older sister, a child of about three years of age. When I spoke to her to give her some attention, she commented, 'He's got no friends.'

There was no receptionist at the desk when I made a follow-up appointment for one lady. We agreed a date and I wrote in down on a card for her which, importantly, contained the words 'Cancellations within twenty-four hours will be charged'. She insisted that she entered it into the diary on her new mobile phone. Over the next ten minutes, she struggled and struggled to perform this entry, while I became more and more frustrated as I had work to do. When eventually she was successful, I bade her goodbye, and just as I was repeatedly banging the heel of my hand against my temple in raw exasperation, she returned to alter the time to another day! 'I cannot get this phone to work,' I said quickly, hoping to defuse the situation.

While I am disclosing embarrassing moments that I would have rather not have happened, as a cautionary tale, I will mention that I treated a formidable lady who was a major TV celebrity. The next patient to arrive was a lady who said that she thought she would be difficult to treat. 'Don't worry,' I said gaily. 'If I can treat XXXX XXXXXXX, I can look after you.'

'Tell me about it,' she said eagerly. 'She is my next-door neighbour.' I learned a salutary lesson that day and NEVER EVER spoke about a patient by name again. I still shudder at this serious lapse of professionalism.

Now that we had a gym with a treadmill, bicycle, parallel bars, wobbleboard and other useful equipment, I felt that we had room for a Cybex machine. This was a large, expensive, cutting-edge piece of kit operated by a computer, which gave the exact amount of resistance to flexion and extension of the knee in order to build up muscle strength. It replaced the pushing and pulling that was back-breaking and tiring for the physios. I negotiated a price to include training in New York and relayed this cost to Hospital Manager (3). 'If anyone goes to New York, then it should be me,' he exclaimed, whereupon I said, 'If you want to treat the sports injuries on the Cybex, that's fine with me.'

So, along with Jenny, the physiotherapy manager from another BUPA hospital, who had purchased a Cybex too as part of this cunning deal, we flew off to New York for a bit of training and a jolly. Life is, after all, what you make it. After three days we were sorry to leave the Big Apple. Then, I asked the company rep to come in and train the staff!

In the new department there was a room with an ultraviolet (UVB) cabinet, like a metal shower cubicle, that patients could stand in. It was used mainly for skin conditions such as acne and psoriasis. One day, a man came down from the skin specialist with a referral for UVB and announced that he had psittacosis. The physio treating him said, 'No, you have psoriasis; psittacosis is a disease that parrots get.' The man was asked to pop on goggles, enter the UVB cabinet and strip off all his clothes to avoid a strip of sunburn if his pants were at different levels as treatment progressed. He was asked to stand with his arms by his sides and call when he was ready. Just as the physio was setting the timer, he opened the cabinet and said, 'Who's a pretty boy?'

A few months later, this same patient had to have surgery to his knee. The ward physio mentioned to us that when she took him for a walk down the corridor, he had a parrot sewn on to the shoulder of his dressing gown. 'Why do you have a parrot on your shoulder?' she asked, as she was a little confused.

'I do not want to look like a wally using crutches,' the droll pirate replied.

Back in the UVB room, another man was given clear instructions but, unbeknown to the physio, kept his hands over his manhood for the first three treatments, then, feeling more confident, he placed his hands at his sides for the next treatment. Unfortunately, this man sustained a very sunburnt penis the week before his wedding. We prescribed after-sun lotion to ease his problem and hoped that his future wife would not arrive and attack us!

Over a course of treatment, we got to know what made our patients tick. It was important to be on the same wavelength so that patients would be compliant. Many opened up to us as we got to know them well during their course of treatment. One guy told me in confidence that he was going to have a special night with his partner. The next day, he came around the corner into the department on his knees! We both laughed uncontrollably.

The physios were told off by the matron for laughing too loudly in the restaurant during our lunch hour. Always happy to oblige, we addressed this by taking only half an hour for lunch (thus reducing the giggles by fifty per cent) and then going home half an hour early.

We treated a number of compensation cases. Possibly the most common were those patients who had suffered whiplash injuries to their necks. Also, many patients suffered from back-related injuries. I had female patients who wore their lumbar corsets over their clothes or always carried back-support cushions wherever they went, in order to make a statement. Some patients carried a walking stick just for effect. The lawyers would request either a photocopy of the patient's notes or a physiotherapy report or both. Unfortunately, many patients who were seeking compensation would consciously or subconsciously make their injuries last until the day that their claim was settled. We could always tell who was malingering. I had one patient with a totally stiff neck seeking a load of compensation, but if I moved out of range while I was chatting to her quietly, she would crane her neck round to hear what I was saying. Our advice to those who wanted to claim for compensation was, 'Avoid the aggravation of legal letters and court appearances and concentrate on getting better.' There is nothing worse than chronic pain, which the brain seems unlikely to forget.

I treated a guy who had pain in his lower leg following an accident at work. He wanted his leg amputated so he could receive considerably more compensation. What a wally! I spoke severely to him about possible phantom pains, the difficulty of prosthetics and the possibility of stump ulcers. I never saw him again. I hope he listened. No amount of money compensates for the loss of a limb.

I assessed a delightful lady once who had backache and when I could find nothing untoward, I asked her, 'When does your back hurt?'

'All the time,' she replied. 'My husband doesn't care for me when I am well, but when I have backache, he is lovely to me, so I always have backache.' What honesty. But how achingly sad.

I was only flummoxed by a patient once. A young weightlifter arrived, saying he would like some ultrasound to his serratus anterior. It was most unusual for a patient to have this detailed knowledge of anatomy. I remembered that this muscle moved the scapula (shoulder blade) forward, but where would I find it? Then I had a brainwave: 'Show me the exact part of serratus anterior that gives you the pain?' I asked, so I was able to treat him accurately. I hope he was impressed.

I refused to treat a patient only once. A young girl came to me with knee pain. She told me that she was suing a physiotherapist from another hospital as she had been touched inappropriately. When I asked her where she was touched, she said, 'On my knee,' so as I could not possibly treat her without touching her leg, I gave her some advice and discharged her. The last thing that I wanted was having to defend myself in court. It was what all physiotherapists dreaded.

I treated another young girl, who bragged about how brilliant she was at writing letters of complaint and gaining compensation. It was no surprise to me that, after she was discharged, Hospital Manager (3) received a well-written letter. Basically, she wanted free treatment. However, she did add as an afterthought that Grace had given her very good care. When I told my manager that she was a professional complainer, he knew just what to write in reply.

We were delighted to have Hospital Manager (4), a well-intentioned manager who,when he was strongly making a point (for the life of me I cannot remember what) and forcing his finger repeatedly onto the desk, saying, 'I am telling you,' I said to him, 'Don't do that, you will hurt your finger.' I never found out why he wanted to reprimand me. I objected to being belittled by a hospital manager; what I needed was a colleague who would be on my side and help me achieve my dream of being the best physiotherapy department in the area. I had the greatest respect for those hospital managers who supported my efforts to give a first-class service to all our patients. Those who would sanction the purchase of equipment, post registration courses for the staff and support my endeavours to expand the department.

I was working on the wards one morning and asked an elderly lady if she would like to walk down the corridor with me. She refused and said that she would report me. 'What is your name?' she asked.

Without thinking, I replied facetiously, 'Petunia.' Fortunately, I never received a complaint about this fictitious physio!

One of my staff told me about an incident that had happened in another hospital and solicited a valid complaint from a patient. The hospital had just bought a new all-singing, all-dancing armchair, which incorporated a seat with a lifting device to help the patient to move from sitting to standing. 'Now you can look out of the window and see the daffodils,' one of the nurses told her. The physio, the ward sister and the matron were all in attendance and watched with horror as the seat ejected this lady onto the floor and she broke both her wrists. Poor lady. I felt for her.

Very few complaints about the staff came to me as physiotherapy manager. One of the patients complained that her physiotherapist talked about her children too much. Most patients only wanted to talk about THEIR problems. Treatment had to be totally patient-centred. Possibly the most embarrassing complaint was when a patient reported that her physiotherapist had body odour and I had to have a gentle word with her about deodorants, antiperspirants and regular washing of her uniform. I hoped her future boyfriends would thank me.

We knew to avoid garlic and strong curries the night before we came on duty, as this could be offensive to some patients (and staff). If only patients complied too.

Each year, I gave each of the staff an appraisal, which mainly consisted of a large pat on the back for all their hard work and enthusiasm. 'Think of all the patients that you have helped this year. They will always remember your kindness,' I used to say. 'I am delighted to have you on the staff.' If I wrote a reference for any of my staff who applied for another job, I would always say that they would be very fortunate to have the applicant in their hospital and that I would re-employ them if they wanted to return to BUPA.

When I had my appraisal, EVERY hospital manager was only interested in the financial figures. I let him know that the physiotherapy department brought in ten per cent of the revenue of the hospital, which was no mean feat, as it included theatres. I also reminded him that the staff worked their socks off providing a high standard of care for their patients. They were a wonderful team. I was so proud of them.

I always felt sorry for deserting the staff when the heads of department went on team-building exercises. Annually, the hospital manager would take us to a swish hotel and we would partake in such activities as clay pigeon shooting or quad bike racing or even, would you believe, making a basket for an egg and throwing it over the hotel! One year, we produced an impromptu pantomime. We scoured the rather smart hotel for costumes and props. I was Goldilocks, but when I tried one of the beds (a cardboard box) for comfort, it collapsed and I went sprawling. Not the best way to build a team!

I wondered if I should take my physio team away for a little team building, but quickly decided that they would prefer the money spent on a pay rise. I went to Hospital Manager (5) to negotiate the annual pay rise. He said that either my staff could have a pay rise or I could have an increase in salary. Either/or! I felt this was most unfair but of course awarded my staff their annual increase, while I fumed at the injustice. I'm still fuming.

I was also interested in staff development. We ran internal courses with each member of staff presenting a topic to the other staff. BUPA would generously pay for their external courses. One physio took her MSc and became a university lecturer. My deputy was successful in gaining a post as a physiotherapy manager in another BUPA hospital. One of the girls left to train to be an osteopath. Many physios went into private practice. I was proud of my team and interested in them and their future careers.

Hospital Manager (5) said that BUPA would pay for me to go on an Open University management course, provided that I passed. The course addressed accountancy and the personal computer, management, and marketing. The tutor reckoned that I had the worst job out of all of the students on the course as I co-ordinated working as a physiotherapist with my managerial role. This was true, as I would appear from a patient's room to be bombarded with management issues such as the lack of a receptionist or staff sickness. Always a challenge. I had never used a computer before, so in the evenings, I started screaming at the screen that I had borrowed from my manager and taught myself by a hit-or-miss approach (mostly miss) to word process. As I had no printer, I saved my work onto a floppy disc and brought it into the hospital for the long-suffering pharmacy manager to unravel and print out. After much frustration and a load of revision, I took the examination and gained the professional certificate of management and, more importantly, received the course fees back from BUPA.

Although I was totally dedicated to my job, sometimes my private life became more important than my working life. One day, I was telephoned by my aunt to say that my cousin had late-stage ovarian cancer. I left for Worthing still in my uniform and stayed with her until she sadly died, then helped my aunt to make all the arrangements.

A few months later, I was sitting happily at the reception desk when I was called to see the skin specialist upstairs. She sat me down and told me gently that my son, Martin, had malignant melanoma on his shoulder following a summer surfing in Cornwall. What a shock. I phoned him with the result and organised an appointment for him to have the lesion completely excised. Within two hours of hearing this bad news,

Rosemary, my sister-in-law, telephoned from Dorset to say that my dear father had a terminal heart condition. The two men in my family were desperately unwell. I sobbed. Immediately, I left the hospital, went home to gather some clothes together and drove down to Dorset. I looked after Pop for three weeks, fending off the regular phone calls from Hospital Manager (5) by saying, 'Even if I lose my job, my place is here with my father.' I stayed down in Dorset until he sadly died.

My dear father, nicknamed Pop, was always a joy to be with. He had worked as a woodwork master for years, taught his three children how to work safely with wood and made sure that each of his six grandchildren had their own toolbox and learned the rudiments of carpentry in his workshop. When I poured out my heart to him and mentioned that I was thinking of divorcing Tony, he said, 'Can't you cope? After all, I have had to put up with your mother for all these years.' I explained that divorce was more acceptable now and that I could be released from living with a man who was mentally and physically abusive and for whom I had lost all respect. After that he was totally supportive. I adored him. Still do.

I came down to visit him in Dorset once and found him sitting at the kitchen table with a hammer and chisel, diligently cutting his pills in half. The next stage was to retrieve the divided pills from the floor! Today there are pill-cutters which deal with this problem.

He became a loose cannon after my mother died and, rather worryingly, took to massaging women from the village because he said, 'My daughter's a physiotherapist,' even though he had never seen me work or been taught by me! I wonder how many ladies he rubbed up the wrong way? You can't be a physiotherapist by proxy!

I took my father (knocking on ninety) to my GP, after he had fallen and injured his head, with a view to preventing him from driving. He (my father, not the doctor) said that he was fortunate because if there was a queue of cars he was always at the front! The understanding GP asked my father all about the vehicles that he had driven, then said, 'I bet you have never had an accident,' to which my father replied, 'No, I have a clean driving record.'

'Let's keep it that way, shall we?' the doctor said obligingly. I was full of admiration for the way my young GP (he was about twelve!) had handled this emotive subject with the right amount of tact and diplomacy. My father announced that he was going to give up 'motoring' there and then. I said that he would save the cost of running a car which would pay for taxis into Dorchester, where he helped out at a seniors' lunch club (and received a hot meal), even though he was years older than most of the members. He also used to attend dances at the village hall, where he made sure that he danced with each lady in turn to avoid disappointing anyone.

My brother, Alan, and my sister, Joyce, and I were worried about Pop falling over again, so we paid for an alarm which would activate if he fell down when he was gardening. He popped it into a spectacle case to stop it going off if he hit the ground but wore it proudly if I was with him! Mobile phones were not available then. Surely, the mobile phone has revolutionised the lives of the elderly, not just for regular communication but for the safety aspect.

Regularly, I used to visit Pop in Dorset and take him to visit his brother and sisters in Bridport, Worthing and Halstead. Each year, I rented a house in South Wales so that I could take my father on holiday. Claire and Martin brought their friends (with sleeping bags) so it was always open house and a hoot. I would buy Pop a copy of the *Daily Telegraph* and then go riding on the beach with the children. His day was complete with a visit to a hardware shop and then taking me out for afternoon tea. It was an absolute pleasure to be with my father.

It took me a good year to get over my father's death. Everyone said you are lucky to have work that you love, but it did not prevent the tears that used to flow at inopportune moments. Once, I was mobilising a lady's cervical spine while she was lying prone and a tear drop fell onto her neck. How sad is that. Sometimes it is hard to be professional.

Occasionally, I would have important calls from home while I was at work. My receptionist told me that my son had telephoned, requesting, 'Please may I speak to Mrs Dorey,' whereupon she replied that I was in a meeting. He then telephoned again, sounding more stressed, and asked, 'Please may I speak to Grace?' to which she answered that she was sorry but I was busy. He then telephoned again with increasing panic: 'Please can I speak to my mum?'

I was duly interrupted in the meeting by the physiotherapy assistant and as we walked quickly back to the department, I said to her, 'This sounds as if it is going to be expensive.' Apparently, Martin had borrowed his sister's 2CV car to go surfing in Devon to celebrate his twenty-first birthday. He had tried to contact her in Hong Kong to ask her permission but had been unable to reach her. Unfortunately, when Martin was on the M5/A361 roundabout, he noticed flames fanning his feet, so he quickly released his seatbelt, jumped out and ran away like an enlightened bomb-disposal officer, leaving the car to become engulfed in flames and then to EXPLODE. As you can imagine, Martin was in shock, but even more so when he found out that his third-party insurance did not include fire and theft! My prediction was correct. It was expensive. I had to buy Claire another car.

We had a succession of young male physios from Australia who used to do the evening clinics for us. We found that the word got around and many of the female patients changed to an evening appointment. Cougars! One day a good-looking Australian physio popped in and asked if there was any work available. He produced a glowing reference, which was far too good to be true. 'Did your mother write this?' I asked him, to which he swiftly replied, 'No, my father did.' I employed him.

The physios had the department to themselves in the evening and one morning I found a list of Australian telephone numbers by the phone. What a giveaway. I addressed this by speaking to the guy involved and then blocking the telephone to and from overseas calls.

I had a feeling that one of the full-time physios was inventing a patient with an appointment at the end of the day, so that when they mysteriously cancelled, the physio could go home early. I admit that I was rather lax and never found the culprit. I trusted my team to give a high standard of care to their patients and when I mentioned this 'clever' idea at our staff meeting, the end-of-day cancellations suddenly stopped.

I used to give the staff a half-day off on Christmas Eve without asking the management. They deserved it. We were delighted that the lovely Jewish staff always covered the on-calls over the Christmas period.

One Christmas Eve, just as I was about to leave, a lady made an urgent appointment to come to see me with acute neck pain as she was travelling to the Midlands for Christmas. When I asked, 'When does your neck hurt?', she got down on the floor and executed a perfectly performed somersault! 'Ah!' I said. 'If you promise not to perform somersaults all the way up the M1, you will be free of pain and you will have a good Christmas.'

I linked together with the physiotherapy managers from all the other BUPA hospitals and set up a valuable support group. We met once a year and exchanged ideas in order to provide a better service for BUPA patients. I instigated a working group to compile a document detailing BUPA physiotherapy standards. Following this, I was nominated for a BUPA Quality Award. No golden trophy, no money, just a worthy mention!

After about ten years of organising the BUPA physiotherapy managers' group, Hospital Manager (5) was brought in to oversee our group. He asked me to step down from this voluntary role, as he knew I felt that we did not need to be organised by a hospital manager. A pretty young physio took over.

Several years later, there was an advertisement for a BUPA physiotherapy co-ordinator at head office. I applied and attended the interview. With the help of Bev, the astute hospital accountant, I put together a cracking PowerPoint presentation which showed that by working together, physiotherapy managers from all the BUPA hospitals could address issues such as recruitment, bulk purchase of equipment, standards and Continuing Professional Development.

Later that day, one of the interviewers telephoned me to let me know that I had been unsuccessful. 'Yours was the best presentation,' he said kindly. 'If it had been ten years ago, you would have walked it.' The other candidate was at least ten years younger. It sounded like ageism. I was fifty-six years of age.

My new hospital manager (6) asked me if I had been successful, so I reported this conversation. 'Do you want me to fight this for you?' he asked.

'No,' I said. 'It is better to leave it.'

While I was working at BUPA, I was elected to serve on the Council of The Chartered Society of Physiotherapy and was released to go to London twice a year for Council meetings. In this capacity as a Council member there was a tranche of reading matter to digest and comment on at the Council meetings. I also served on three committees with even more papers to read: the Ethical and Regulatory Committee, which advised the Council of the need for updating standards and rules; the Preliminary Committee, which identified members who had strayed from the rules of professional conduct and, after a fair hearing, could be struck off (most complainants were women who felt they had been touched inappropriately when they had been manipulated, even though they were held in a correct and professional manner); and the Awards Committee, which recommended to the Council the members who should be awarded a Fellowship of The Chartered Society of Physiotherapy. At this committee I was incensed that many physios fell short of the strict criteria needed to gain a Fellowship and were therefore not recognised for their contribution to physiotherapy. I suggested that there should be another award for those physios who had given exemplary service to the profession, so with the agreement from all the committee members and eventually ratified by the Council, the Distinguished Service Award was born.

In 1994, the Chartered Society of Physiotherapy held its hundred-year celebrations in Birmingham, where I met HRH Prince Charles, who said that he was most impressed with the exhibition showing all aspects of physiotherapy.

'It should be good,' I said to him. 'It has taken us a hundred years to put this on for you!' He had done his homework, as he mentioned that Australian physiotherapists trained for four years instead of three years in the UK.

There was also a celebratory church service in London where I bumped into little Miss Orme, who seemed to have shrunk even further, or was that because I was wearing high heels? 'What are you doing now, Miss Blundell?' she asked.

'I am at BUPA Hospital Bushey, where they have just made me quality manager,' I replied, to which she emphasised, 'Standards, standards, standards, I have always said, standards, Miss Blundell.'

At the Council, I waved the flag for physiotherapists who worked in private hospitals. At that time, there was a feeling that NHS physiotherapists were more dedicated and that physios who abandoned the NHS were working in better conditions (with carpets) and receiving a higher salary. Yes, we had private rooms for our patients; yes, there was no waiting list, but we worked evening shifts, weekends and were on call too. Also, our salary was commensurate with NHS physios. I regularly reminded the NHS physios that The Chartered Society of Physiotherapy supported their members wherever they worked.

What I cherished most in the private sector was that we had enough TIME to assess, diagnose and treat our patients. Also, they came to us soon after their initial injury (without having to wait weeks for an appointment), so it was easier to help them before their symptoms became chronic. They enjoyed coming to an aesthetically pleasing department and being treated individually by SENIOR physiotherapists.

My colleague Claire set up a new group titled the Association of Chartered Physiotherapists in Independent Hospitals which became affiliated to The Chartered Society of Physiotherapy. I was elected secretary and when Claire retired, I was elected president. This group included physios who worked in independent hospitals and clinics, the armed services and charities. It addressed issues such as working conditions, salaries, standards and further training. BUPA management were very suspicious of this group and were worried that their physios would become militant. We had to reassure them that it was advantageous for us to work together.

I was invited to be quality manager for the hospital to steer us through ISO 9002. This took an increased workload for all the already busy departmental heads and I think was time poorly spent. Through hard work and multiple document writing (a ridiculous amount), we did gain this prestigious award, but as far as patients were concerned, they came to us because we had a good reputation and gave everyone quality care. The next year Hospital Manager (6) relieved me of this burden and brought in two full-time staff and two secretaries to deal with the mountain of paperwork, and I happily returned to physiotherapy.

Then, BUPA had the bright idea of staff ranking the effectiveness of their managers. That is when I entered with a large bag of donuts before asking my staff to kindly complete the forms. When I saw Hospital Manager (6), who was my immediate boss (I refused to be under the matron), he showed me my rather impressive ratings before feebly showing me his chart. 'I can see where you went wrong,' I said. 'You failed to give your staff donuts before they filled in the forms!'

I was unable to find a specialist continence physiotherapist for all the patients needing help with urinary leakage. The staff ganged up on me. They thought that as I had given birth to two babies, I would be best placed to take this work on. I could tell that this was not an area that floated their boat. They preferred to treat young men with sports injuries (and young women, if push came to shove). So, I found out about a residential continence course in Bradford and swiftly joined their programme.

I learned about stress urinary incontinence, urge urinary incontinence and faecal incontinence in women. We were shown how to perform a vaginal examination and rate the strength of the pelvic floor muscles from Grade 0 (no muscle movement) to Grade 5 (a strong muscle contraction). We were shown various vaginal probes for delivering electrical stimulation in order to gain a muscle contraction. This pulsed electrical stimulation treatment was comfortable and nothing like the uncomfortable spikey faradism that our poor patients had been exposed to previously. We were shown how to use the interferential machine to crossfire the pelvic floor muscles to gain a contraction, but I found this treatment was ineffective and not nearly as helpful as electrical stimulation with a vaginal probe. We were also shown a brilliant biofeedback machine for monitoring the strength of the muscle contraction. These treatments were always followed up with pelvic floor exercises.

We were given a continence pad to try. I was rather slow so picked the last pad out of the bin liner. It was HUGE. The lecturer said, 'Those with the large pads, try peeing now.' I could no more pass urine onto a pad than fly to the moon. It gave me so much more empathy for patients who were given pads by nurses in hospital to stop them from wetting the bed, instead of taking the time and trouble to take them to the toilet.

The course included preparing case studies, presentations and visits to other professionals, and the keeping of a reflective diary over six months. For the diary, we had to write on one page about our successes or failures in treating continence patients and six months later we had to reflect on what we had learned using a different-coloured pen on the opposite page. I admit (possibly unwisely in a book) that I sat down and wrote this diary in one day and felt guilty when I received the highest mark for this fictional account!

I went on two statutory visits. Firstly, I sat in on a gynaecologist's clinic. There, I can vividly remember seeing a complete prolapse of the womb hanging down, like an ulcerated phallus, between this poor lady's legs and being appalled that she had suffered from it for six months without complaining, believing that it was one of the hazards of giving birth. She was referred for immediate surgery.

I also made an appointment to see the local sex therapist, who rather unprofessionally charged me to sit in on her clinic. After a day off, I went back into my office and found a notice the size of a sheet of A3 spread across my desk: 'YOUR APPOINTMENT WITH THE SEX THERAPIST HAS BEEN CHANGED TO TUESDAY'. I never let on that I was going to see her as part of the continence course, so I reckoned my staff would have to wonder for ever (until now!).

There, I saw a young lady who had got married to get away from her abusive father. She arrived with her husband, who said that after a year of marriage, when he touched her, she recoiled in fear. He demonstrated this in front of the therapist. How sad for both of them. The couple were given light massage and cuddling homework (the best type of homework) and asked to return in a month.

Next, a transvestite arrived with his wife, who complained that her husband paid more for his handbags and make-up than she did. A kind of domestic dispute.

Then, another man arrived and was asked to sit down in the clinic while the therapist looked for his notes. She was away ages and I felt most uncomfortable being in the same room as him, as I had no idea why he was attending the clinic. He could have been a sexual predator for all I knew. *After* she had seen him, I was told that there was a panic button under her desk.

In the department, the physios were encouraged to press the cardiac arrest button if they were threatened or assaulted by a patient. I can remember treating a chap one morning early and performing mobilisation to his painful shoulder. All too innocently, I said, 'You can shout if you like, as there is no-one here this early.' Before he left he stood with his back to the door and asked me for his Christmas kiss. I froze and said firmly, 'No way.'

We were mindful that presents from patients could be seen as bribes. We accepted chocolates, of course, but were expected to pass money over to the hospital. After a course of treatment, patients wanted to thank their physio, so it would have been churlish to refuse the odd bottle of plonk or even gift of champagne. That said, we used our discretion and in order not to offend, we accepted small gifts and expressed our gratitude.

One of the physios was offered the keys of a Mercedes Benz sports car by a patient if she would go out with him. She refused politely. The Chartered Society of Physiotherapy was quite clear in those days; we could not date a patient whom we were treating. If we met them after they were discharged this was allowed.

One day, a handsome man entered the department at 12.30pm and asked if anyone could treat him. 'I am free,' I heard myself say, so I took him into the cubicle and treated the skiing injury to his knee. All my staff instantly knew that I fancied him as I NEVER EVER treated anyone at lunchtime! Nick was a patient with a brilliant brain and an exquisite turn of phrase, whose uniqueness was beguiling. I looked forward to his attendances.

When he was better, I discharged him and he invited me to have free lessons at the dry ski slope, as I was shortly going skiing for the first time. I was fairly hopeless so needed lessons each Sunday. I wore skiwear and packed a bag of going-to-dinner clothes (and a toothbrush), which were never needed.

After I returned from the skiing holiday, Nick popped into the physio department and asked me if I would like to tell him about my holiday over a drink and our relationship began. That was thirty-four years ago.

A physio friend asked me if I would see her father-in-law when I returned from the Bradford continence course, so I booked him an appointment. I said to him, 'I have learned all about women, but the course failed to mention men's problems.' As he was a GP, he brought in copies of *The Lancet* and the *British Medical Journal*, and we learned together. He stimulated my interest in men's conditions and when I wrote my first textbook a few years later, I dedicated it to this fine man.

After being stimulated by the Bradford course, I wanted to explore the continence issues in men, so I enrolled at the University of East London to take an MSc by independent study. I attended the university once a week over a two-year period. It was exhausting travelling to East London, a journey which took two hours each way after work, and then studying in the evening and at weekends. For my thesis, I contacted all the physios from around the world, who were treating male patients with continence issues and brought together a best treatment plan using their ideas. I also designed a male continence assessment form. As part of my MSc examination, I gave a lecture to physios and nurses on post-prostatectomy incontinence, using photographic slides that I had made in the days before PowerPoint presentations. I was examined by one external and two internal examiners and given a pass rate of seventy-eight per cent. Both internal examiners immediately called me at home and asked me to request a remark, as they felt that I should have been given eighty per cent and been commended. 'Don't worry, I am going to continue studying and work for a doctorate,' I replied.

The MSc award ceremony was held at the Barbican, and for the first time I wore a cap and gown. When I trained at The London Hospital, I only gained a diploma, so I felt rather proud when I was dressed up in front of Nick (my lunchtime patient), my daughter, Claire, and son, Martin. The London Hospital School of Physiotherapy became the North East London Polytechnic and began a degree course in 1981. In 1992, it became the University of East London and I was delighted when, in that year, physiotherapy became an all-graduate profession.

Out of the blue, as thanks for serving on the Council of The Chartered Society of Physiotherapy, I was invited to attend a garden party at Buckingham Palace with another Council member and two of The Chartered Society of Physiotherapy staff. Fortunately, the day was sunny and warm, but we should have arrived earlier as we found all the chairs had already been filled. People were queueing ten deep to see the Queen and, due to my short stature, and without someone's shoulders to sit on, I had no chance to see who was in the royal party. We did, however, wander round the gardens and viewed the wildflower meadow by the lake. The taxi could not have come soon enough, as my new pink shoes, bought to match the stylish new outfit I had bought in an exclusive charity shop (the Queen may well have seen it before!) were killing my feet and I couldn't wait to take them off. I kicked them off in the cab. The relief from the pain was the best part of the day!

At this time, I had pain of another kind. I awoke at night with acute pain under my ribs which only settled if I threw up. Very unpleasant. Despite these nocturnal episodes, I still worked during the day as if nothing was amiss. After a particularly painful night, I decided that I should do something about it, so popped upstairs (in the hospital, not at home!) to see the gastroenterologist, who diagnosed gallstones and suggested surgery, which I promptly refused. Apparently, he said to his nurse, 'She'll be back,' and within a week I was pleading with him to operate immediately. BUPA gave their staff medical insurance, so I was able to be admitted straight away to a smart en-suite room in my own hospital just in time for Wimbledon fortnight. How clever was that! I had a routine cholecystectomy and delivered a gallstone the size of a grape. It was squinting at me in a little jar when I woke up. The surgeon was still practising his keyhole skills on a pig, so said he would do a routine operation as didn't want me to be a guinea pig! I was given three months off work and caught up with my friends who were not working. In fact, we would meet for lunch (and wine) and I would sleep for the afternoon. A very pleasant way to convalesce! When it was time to return to work, the staff had left an arrangement of flowers for me on my desk as a welcome back. So kind and thoughtful. Aren't physios wonderful?

Exactly a year later (yes, Wimbledon fortnight was just beginning – funny that!), I was having gynaecological problems. At 'the change', women either shrivel up inside or bleed to death. I fell into the latter camp and worked diligently on, being fearful of staining my white uniform, until I decided that enough was enough and that I should be sensible and sort myself out. I made an appointment to see the gynaecologist and he recommended a vaginal hysterectomy. I was pleased that my medical insurance meant that I could be admitted straight away, which is how it should be for EVERY patient needing surgery, either privately or on the NHS. This time post-operatively, I had a morphine pump so I could administer my own pain relief. When the nurses compared the amount that they had injected the previous year, they found that I had used much less painkiller when I was in charge of my own pain control. One evening, Nick brought a banquet in for the night nurses, so we had a party in my room, which elicited a complaint from the patient in the next-door room, so she was invited to join in the fun too! I spent the summer convalescing on full pay with my friends and all too soon it was time to return to work.

Much later, I had surgery for the varicose veins in both legs which were bulging, causing my ankles to swell and throb when I was standing for any length of time. I had inherited this problem from my mother and possibly a tranche of knobbly-legged forebears. Ever since I had surgery, my legs have been pain-free and the thrombophlebitis has disappeared, but afterwards, on long-haul flights over four hours, to prevent thrombosis sneaking up, I insisted on travelling business class. The downside of this operation was that the veins of my lower legs could not be harvested for heart bypass surgery, but I was not to find out about that until much later.

While I am on a health kick, much later on, I had a small operation under sedation for de Quervain's tenosynovitis when the tendon of my thumb became too painful to allow me to write my patients' notes. Any time I caught my thumb when dressing, bathing or in my pocket, I would flinch in agony. The surgeon cleverly opened up the sheath to my thumb tendon and performed a miracle, as it has not given me any discomfort since. Thank goodness for modern-day surgery.

At twenty years after we qualified from The London Hospital (called The Royal London Hospital since 1990), I thought it would be good for our set to have a reunion. I called The Chartered Society of Physiotherapy and asked for the married names and addresses of the fifteen physios with whom I had completed my training and whose consecutive numbers they held. I drew a blank. They could not possibly give away such well-guarded secrets. Eventually, I found that one physio knew another, who had kept in touch with another and gradually we traced everyone. We have held a reunion every year since, with a special celebration dinner with our other halves for our fifty-year anniversary. This year we celebrated sixty years since we started training. Sadly, there are only eleven physios on the list now out of an original set of fifteen who qualified. At our reunions we always remember our dear friends who are no longer with us. We have fond memories of Meriel, Rosemary, Rocca and Gill, who were brilliant physiotherapists and treasured friends.

These reunions are one of the highlights of my year. We laugh, compare notes, exchange memories and proudly show photographs. Over the years, we have been shown wedding photos, baby photos, school photos, our children's wedding photos and, of course, pictures of our beloved grandchildren. We have discussed everything from giving birth, to our working lives, hysterectomies, poor health and now the freedom of retirement. Oh, and how imaginatively we are spending our children's inheritance!

I had worked at BUPA Hospital Bushey for seventeen years and spoke to my friend Bev, the accounts manager and found that I could tap into my BUPA pension if I retired at fifty-eight years, so I spoke to Hospital Manager (6): 'If I leave two years early, you will recruit a physio on a lower salary and save £5,000 over a two-year period, so how about paying me this amount to leave?' He must have liked my impertinence, or perhaps he wanted me to go, because he agreed, provided I gave him a letter to include the workings of this 'canny' deal. What a hero!

I went down to Devon and met my son, Martin, and we made appointments to view three cottages at two o'clock, three o'clock and four o'clock. My requirements were for a period property, a stunning view, a large farmhouse kitchen and, most importantly, NOT accessed by a myriad of winding lanes. I fell in love with the four o'clock property and put in a cheeky offer which was accepted.

Two weeks later, I sold my house in Chesham Bois while I was at a conference in Monaco and prepared to move. BUPA heads of department took me out to dinner and the hospital staff gave me a wonderful celebration in the gym with many thoughtful presents. Unashamedly, I am including the speech from one of my kind physios:

'What I am going to say about Grace will be brief but, I feel, important. It is certainly heartfelt.

'I have known Grace professionally for about five and a half years. What I have admired about her most during that time is her absolute dedication to her staff – to their professional and, more rarely these days, to their personal needs. The ever-increasing demands of modern business life makes so many institutions impersonal. Individuals and their needs often come to the bottom of the pile in the drive for greater efficiency. It demands courage, therefore, on the part of those in positions of responsibility to maintain their human dignity in the face of these pressures. Grace has that courage. Many of us can give examples of the sympathetic way in which she has handled her staff. Many of those examples are private and personal, and only Grace knows how many they are. Those who know her well can guess. We have always felt that we come first as people, not simply as employees. These observations are not clichés – they are entirely appropriate. We shall remember you, Grace, as a compassionate and caring human being, and we can pay you no greater compliment.'

WOW! This physio could be a speechwriter.

Chapter 7

Research

I moved to Devon and, after having joined the tennis club, I enrolled at the University of the West of England, Bristol to study for a PhD exploring the use of pelvic floor exercises for men with erectile dysfunction. At the interview, one of the lecturers asked why I was only given seventy-eight per cent for my masters at the University of East London, as they would ALWAYS make it up to eighty per cent. I mentioned that I had been advised to get it remarked but considered it unimportant as I wished to study for a doctorate. I was accepted as a PhD student.

Then, I found quite by accident that student houses were exempt from paying council tax, so my quaint sixteenth-century cottage quickly became a student house and I paid no rates for three years. That was quite a saving! My fees at the university were paid by a medical company, which kindly sponsored me and to whom I am eternally grateful. I restored my barn and let it to holidaymakers for extra income so somehow made ends meet.

I worked mainly at home, attending a meeting with my clinical tutors once a month at the university in Bristol. I studied seven days a week. I saw no friends. I read no books, newspapers or magazines unless they were related to my field of study. Medical papers were becoming available on the internet, so I didn't have to trawl through the journal article references at the library as I had done for my MSc. The difficulty was narrowing the field of study to just the relevant articles.

I bought Mischa, a Golden Retriever, from my neighbour Glennis, and when my neck and shoulders were sore from pounding the computer keyboard, I ran her round the block or over the fields. Often, I would start the day writing while still in my dressing gown. Doesn't everybody? I felt that I was on a treadmill and couldn't let up until I had finished.

It was a busy time. I was elected to a number of committees such as the Association for Continence Advice, the Chartered Physiotherapists Promoting Continence and the Association of Chartered Physiotherapists in Women's Health, to which I wanted desperately to add 'and Men's Health'. I served for a number of years but found that the journey to London became too time-consuming. I left this important work to the younger physios.

Once a month I had a clinic at the Queen's Pelvic Centre on the corner of Harley Street. I enjoyed working there enormously and if I am honest, I quite liked the Harley Street address, but found the travelling to and from London too exhausting.

With the handsome gynaecologist Mr Seumas Eckford, I set up the continence clinic at the North Devon District Hospital Ladywell Unit in Barnstaple and I worked there two mornings a week for several years. I thoroughly enjoyed the work there, treating women for a range of continence problems. At times, I was able to sneak a few male patients into this setting, as there was no physiotherapist treating male continence problems.

Although I worked for only six hours a week, I had to attend all the NHS mandatory lectures with the full-time staff. I happily attended the fire, resuscitation, health and safety and infection control lectures, but I baulked at attending the safeguarding children lecture, as I only treated adults, and I positively refused to attend the manual handling lecture, as I used to be the staff trainer for this discipline at BUPA (I even made a training video for them, which they confiscated as it hadn't been made by their marketing department). Ridiculously, I had to provide a separate police disclosure for each place in which I worked (Somerset Nuffield, North Devon and Queen's). Why in the name of common sense couldn't the same disclosure be used for all three! They all related to me. Why! I felt that all the red tape was strangling me and taking me away from my first love of treating patients. Eventually, I left because first of all, staff were charged for using the car park and secondly, after work my car was often hemmed in and I was unable to get to tennis in time. A girl has to have priorities.

I was offered a job at the Somerset Nuffield Hospital in Taunton by the wonderful physiotherapy manager, Ros, who invited me to start a continence clinic. I persuaded the hospital to purchase a biofeedback machine and used this for my research patients. Men from the NHS were delighted to be treated free at a private hospital. For my research I had two groups of men who had not undergone prostate surgery: those who were randomly selected into the intervention group, who received pelvic floor exercises with biofeedback and lifestyle changes such as getting fit, losing weight, ceasing smoking and limiting alcohol; and those who were selected into the control group, who received only lifestyle changes.

Biofeedback was delivered using a balloon anal probe covered with a condom liberally smeared with KY jelly. All the men understood why I needed to monitor their pelvic floor muscle strength and all but one appeared happy with their treatment. This apprehensive guy, whose wife insisted on accompanying him, winced when I gently inserted the small, lubricated anal probe. I felt that he was sending a message to her! Although the men could have their partner present, I preferred to treat the men who were unaccompanied.

These men were a delight to treat; I used to sit on the plinth holding the probe in the anal canal with my left hand while my right hand was working the dials on the biofeedback machine to ascertain their pelvic floor strength. Unfortunately, one time I was sitting there, the foot end of the plinth gave way and I slowly slid down the slope until I landed on the floor wedged firmly against the wall. The anal probe popped out like a champagne cork and the patient commented, 'Where have you gone?' It was extremely difficult getting up from the floor with the soiled probe held aloft. Fortunately, my patient also had a wry sense of humour and we laughed at this calamity.

Fifty-five men, who had not undergone prostate surgery, were recruited into the trial; twenty-eight were randomised into the intervention group and twenty-seven into the control group.

The men in the active group started to improve and many regained normal erectile function after three months of biofeedback and pelvic floor exercises in the clinic, followed by a further three months of home pelvic floor exercises. I gave a questionnaire to the men to give to their partners and had to make a note of whether the partner was their wife or lover so that I did not put my foot in it. Many of the wives sent me thank-you cards. The lovers kept schtum. After three months the men in the control group failed to improve. I felt sorry for them as they had missed out, so I offered them the intervention for three months, followed by three months of home pelvic floor exercises.

The results were STUNNING. Out of all the men who had received pelvic floor exercises, forty per cent regained normal erectile function, a further thirty-five per cent gained improved erectile function, but unfortunately twenty-five per cent failed to improve. From the data, the younger men had a better chance of improving compared to the older men. Also, men taking anti-hypertensive medication (for high blood pressure) were in the group who failed to improve. Other failures included a charming man with no testicles, a professional cyclist (affected by constant saddle pressure), those who had smoked for years (smoking makes all the small blood vessels contract) and a couple of exceptionally heavy drinkers (brewer's droop).

In the same trial, I also evaluated the use of pelvic floor exercises for men with post-micturition dribble, i.e. men who dribbled urine when they walked away from the toilet. I found that after pelvic floor exercises, ALL these men prevented any dribble by tightening their pelvic floor muscles UP strongly while they were still poised over the bowl (their previous tendency was to push down and force the last few drops out, instead of tightening UP their sphincter to turn the tap off).

After three years of intensive study, I finished my thesis and presented the university with a copy each for one external examiner and two internal examiners. Also, I added a textbook that I had written while studying titled '*Conservative Treatment of Male Urinary Incontinence and Erectile Dysfunction*' and a self-help book for men titled '*Use It or Lose It*' in order to impress. I tied each examiner's offering up with red ribbon to resemble a present. The university gave me a bottle of champagne, as it was unheard of for a student to complete a PhD in under three years!

My viva was challenging. (I heard afterwards that it is possible to gain a PhD by writing a textbook and defending its contents. SHUCKS!) During the viva, I felt the examiners were trying to assert their superior knowledge in front of their colleagues. I felt an axe go through my head when one of the internal examiners said that I should have analysed my statistics using non-parametric tests instead of parametric. When I said that my statistician had suggested that I analysed the results in this way, he said, 'You should sack your statistician.' WHOA!

I was asked to sit outside the room while the examiners deliberated. After sitting outside the door for what seemed like a week (a bad sign) while the examiners considered their verdict, they called me in. They stood up and I thought, *This has to be bad*. The head examiner congratulated me on passing my PhD as long as I reanalysed my data. So, I sat down with Paul, my sterling 'non-sacked' statistician, my saviour, and did just that! (Paul said that they expected me to know information that was learned on the third year of a statistics degree.)

Thus, after three years of in-depth study where I had contributed to the body of knowledge in a narrow but important specialist area, I became a doctor. Doctor Dorey: it had a nice ring to it! Proudly, I sent a group email to all my friends, saying, 'Trust me, I'm a doctor!' It felt good. The first Christmas I got rather sniffy if family and friends still sent me cards to Mrs Dorey instead of my well-earned title: Dr Dorey! Since then I have not been quite so critical! Once, my new title came in handy when I had food poisoning and I took the soup container back to Tesco and reported my problem. The acting manager quizzed me rather unsympathetically: 'Have you seen a doctor?', whereupon I replied, with enough confidence to melt the hardest heart, 'I am a doctor!'

ALL of the national press covered the results of my research and I went on local BBC TV in Bristol. I noticed that the interviewer had his face powdered, but this service was not open to his guests! In recognition of my work, I was awarded a research prize from the Nuffield Foundation, a Best Presentation Award from the UK branch of the International Continence

Society, which included a very welcome generous cheque, and a fellowship from The Chartered Society of Physiotherapy. A wonderful honour. Wow!

My fellowship presentation was at The Chartered Society of Physiotherapy's annual conference in Leicester. I donned a blue robe, lifted up my skirt so that it did not hang below my gown and walked onto the stage where the chair of Council conferred this honour. I did shed a tear as this was an awesome accolade, certainly something that I never ever expected. Afterwards, I had dinner with the kind physios who had so generously nominated me for this award. I was so grateful. I wanted to pay the bill, but my colleagues would not let me even think about it. Physios are so kind and thoughtful.

My PhD ceremony took place in the impressive setting of Bristol Cathedral. I was asked by one guest, 'Why are you wearing a red robe while everyone else is wearing a black one?'

'I am so glad that you asked that,' I replied. 'The red robe and this floppy hat are for a PhD.' That year, there were only two doctors in red: a young girl who was there with her daughter while I was there with my granddaughter! Nick, Claire, Martin, his wife Jo and my granddaughter Maggie, aged just one year, came to the ceremony. Then my tutor announced from the pulpit, 'I would like to commend pelvic floor exercises to the congregation.' The audience clapped until I had walked the length of the cathedral. It was deafening. I was beyond ecstatic, possibly unbearable!

The University of the West of England invited me to present a doctoral lecture to staff from the university and invited guests in a steep old-fashioned lecture theatre. Just before I commenced my lecture, the dean came up to me and said, 'We would like to make you a visiting professor.' How do you give a presentation after that! I started very timidly trying not to blow my future chances, but soon forgot as I rather proudly presented the serendipitous results of my research. After the lecture, I took my friends and family out to the local Chinese restaurant and we celebrated together. WOW! What a day. I was floating…

Six months after I became Dr Dorey, I became Professor Dorey, a title I could never have imagined was possible when I flung myself onto my bed all those years ago. I had left school having failed two A-levels, had found physiotherapy training physically demanding, had struggled to cope with what I considered was misplaced authority from the bosses in my first two jobs, had a marriage which had failed, had tried to be a fair and reasonable physiotherapy manager, had earned my PhD after three years' hard graft and now, to top it all, I had become a visiting university professor. How had it happened?

I came from a teaching family: my mother started a nursery school with her three children and two of our friends, which grew exponentially to provide schooling for a hundred privileged infants who graduated at the age of five; my father was a gifted woodwork and metalwork master; my brother taught engineering; and my sister was a deputy head of a junior school. As a feisty teenager with boundless energy, I felt that I would prefer to 'do something' rather than teach, so it was a huge surprise to me, when I was learning exciting new information in my newfound speciality, that I wanted to share it with my colleagues, first by writing it down in a textbook and then by spreading the word by lecturing face to face. PowerPoint was a brilliant educational tool. I loved creating the lectures with up-to-date information and recent research coupled with the occasional cartoons and comments to make the delegates smile. Education had to be fun so that they remembered the content or, at the very least, were kept awake.

I presented my professorial lecture to the vice-dean, lecturers from the university and an invited audience in a large hall in the university. I titled my lecture 'Under Every Good Man' and started by indicating that under every good man there could be a horse, a pogo stick, a pedestal (for consultants?) or a pelvic floor. Everything went well until I showed a slide which I had just downloaded from the European Association of Urology textbook which showed a penis adorned with multiple ring piercings, which I was happy to share with the invited guests. Talk about bells and whistles! I said, 'Can you imagine meeting that on a dark night?' Then I added innocently, 'But at least you would hear him coming.' WHOOPS! I can still hear the roar of spontaneous sexual laughter. Of dear, what would Miss Orme say? I breathed in, recovered my professional image and continued with anatomy, physiology and my stunning research findings, and concluded, 'Under every man there may be a horse, a pogo stick, or a pedestal, but under every good man is a PHYSIOTHERAPIST.'

After I presented my professorial lecture, the vice-dean said to the head of the faculty, 'You cannot let this one go.' I had done something right. So, I was invited to an interview for a professorial post one day a week. The interviewer started by letting me know that this was just a formality (phew!), then he asked me, 'What is more important to you, men's incontinence or their erectile dysfunction?' Oh dear, what a question!

I replied, 'I am afraid that I am unable to answer this question as they are equally important.' We talked about what I could bring to the faculty, so I agreed to give lectures to the physio students and bring my female continence study day and my male continence study day in house to the university. We agreed that my new title would be Professor of Physiotherapy (Urology). Wow!

In this capacity, I lectured to students at the university about female and male continence. When I finished the first lecture, a male student came up to me and said, 'That was the best lecture that I have ever attended.' What a cool chap to bother to give feedback and kindly make my day. I did have a tangible reward, though, as with the earnings from my new post, I built an extension to my sixteenth-century cottage, which I named the 'Professorial Conservatory'.

I became a clinical tutor to chartered physiotherapist Kay Crotty, a PhD student at the University of Hertfordshire and my proudest moment was seeing her, after a gruelling ten years of study, become a doctor in a colourful ceremony in St Albans Abbey. Also, I became a clinical supervisor to a successful PhD physiotherapist in Sydney (all by email).

I examined a successful PhD physio from Melbourne, but was disappointed when I was told that there was no viva for me to attend in Australia, just the thesis to mark! I examined and this time attended the viva of a successful nurse who gained a PhD in Cornwall.

I was delighted to play a small role in the achievement of these students – two as clinical tutor and two as an examiner – and I felt proud that the knowledge I had gained in my chosen speciality was helping others to fly.

Chapter 8

International Lecturer

While I was studying, I developed a male continence study day to train physiotherapists and nurses about the theory and practice of assessing and treating men with urinary leakage. Often, this was one of the unfortunate side effects of prostate surgery and radiotherapy. Naturally, I also took the opportunity to talk about the use of pelvic floor exercises for men with erectile problems.

Nick bought me a portable computer for my sixtieth birthday, a most welcome present, so I could travel with my precious PowerPoint lectures to each venue as there were too many diagrams, pictures and cartoons to be able to fit onto a floppy disk. When USB (Universal Serial Bus) devices came out, it was a godsend to carry this small gadget around without the need to transport a computer, leads and plug. I always travelled with two USBs, one in my handbag and one in my suitcase, just to make sure!

I made a CD to show how to perform a correct digital anal examination wearing non-latex gloves and lots of KY lubrication. I encouraged a company who made plastic models to make a model of the male pelvis, complete with the correct musculature, for use as a teaching tool for students and patients. I found it rather tiring holding a different plastic model of a man's pelvis complete with penis and testicles and anus, and then pumping up the muscles for twenty delegates, while they each perfected the anal examination.

I only had one student leave before I finished a study day. This physio strongly objected when I mentioned that electrical stimulation was important to show patients how to perform pelvic floor exercises, but it did not strengthen the muscles like a programme of regular strong pelvic floor exercise. She wanted a passive treatment for her patients. I was disappointed that she did not wait to hear my views. Her colleagues were adamant that they would inform her manager that she had left before lunch.

I used to be asked a variety of questions during these study days, but by far the most frequent was, 'Do men ever get an erection when you are treating them?' I honestly said that this had never happened to any of the men during their treatment. Historically, physiotherapists treating men had asked them to wrap their 'naughty bits' in a towel and performed an anal examination when they were in a side-lying position. However, I examined men lying with just a paper towel over their abdomen as I needed to see the penile dip and scrotal lift, which happened when they were performing pelvic floor exercises correctly. Initially, this lift would be sluggish, but as they improved there was a much speedier contraction with increased movement. No-one refused an examination. However, ALL the men were concerned about their penis size. When they asked me directly, I said that they were BIG. How do I know?

I also ran a female continence study day, where delegates would learn about the female anatomy, birth injuries, prolapses and the different types of leakage. I taught physios to perform a vaginal examination using a female plastic model where I could pump up the muscles to simulate the varying strength of the pelvic floor muscles. I also explained that the pelvic floor muscles were active during orgasm.

I ran a female continence study day on a blistering hot day in Bushey and covered anatomy, physiology, types of continence, the current research and a practical on performing a vaginal examination. I always included a continence knowledge quiz to show the delegates how much they had learned on the course. I finished the day giving a lecture on pelvic floor exercises for achieving sexual fulfilment, which they always enjoyed. The French windows were open to bring a breeze into the room, but the curtains were closed so that delegates could see the screen. During the lecture, I disclosed to the students that for Easter I had been given a heart-shaped tin box by my partner, which obviously contained chocolates. When I opened it, there were not chocolates but there was a plastic egg the size of a pullet's egg which vibrated using a remote switch. I told them that I had popped it into my vagina when I went to a dinner party. My partner kept the switch in his pocket and during the meal I felt, in no uncertain terms, that he was thinking of me!

Then the curtain over the French window billowed and showed that my partner was standing there waiting to give me a lift back home! He had obviously heard my indiscrete comments about our relationship! I blushed bright red and was totally unable to finish the lecture. Everyone snorted with laughter when I told them that they would have to read the last few slides on their own! One delegate called out, 'I have never seen you at a loss for words.' I think I must report that Nick and I giggled all the way home.

Interestingly, about ten years previously, I attended my first continence lecture, and heard the lecturer speaking quite freely about the intimate female anatomy without a hint of embarrassment. I was full of admiration for her confident approach. And now here I was, giving a study day using medical terms for the bits and pieces 'down there' without a hint of embarrassment. Until now...

To date, I have given a hundred of these study days in the UK and abroad. I have been lucky enough to be invited to lecture in Ireland, France, Spain, Portugal, Holland, Germany, Canada, America, Norway, Denmark, Sweden, Finland, Singapore, Hong Kong, Iceland, Australia, Tasmania and New Zealand. In fact, in most of the English-speaking countries. By far the worst study day I presented was in Spain, where their English was poor and they had to use a translator. I would say a few words, then the translator spoke. He could have said anything; how was I to know? It meant that I shortened my lectures and cut out all the interesting asides and funnies that make the day more interesting. It would have been much better to have had instantaneous translation.

The first time that my lecture was translated was in France. I showed one cartoon with a caption and the English-speaking delegates laughed; this was followed, after a short pause, by a chuckle from the French, who obviously have a delayed sense of humour!

Interestingly, I have just heard about an earpiece which has been developed by two brilliant scientists from China, which receives speech in one language and then gives instantaneous translation into another one. This innovation could revolutionise travel abroad and communication with people from other countries. At the moment, the International Continence Society's proceedings are always in English, which means that foreigners only take part if they are able to understand and speak English well. This precludes many deserving delegates from attending these conferences. If these earpiece gadgets were available to those who needed them either at a fair price or could be rented cheaply, many more professionals from abroad could hear about the cutting-edge research that is presented each year. This is another example of how modern technology can help medicine to evolve.

I stayed with Anna, a delightful physio in Canada, where I presented a male continence study day. Afterwards, she took me to Vancouver Island and the Rocky Mountains, where we went for a walk over a footbridge in a forested area and saw a cute baby black bear. Ah! However, this bundle of loveliness was followed closely by its mother, who was the size of a furry black taxi and ten times as intimidating. We stood stock still. Our exit over the bridge was blocked by the massive bear, so we held hands (and our breaths) while our hearts raced off the scale as we waited nervously for her to either attack us or disappear into the forest. Once they had wandered off without seeing or smelling us, we silently (apart from the noise of our hearts thumping) tiptoed back to the safety of the car. It was a brush with nature that I shall never forget. Anna dined out on the story in Canada.

Following the success of my research, I was asked to present my findings to physios in every city in Australia, Tasmania and New Zealand. It was the first time that the Australian Physiotherapy Association had co-ordinated lectures across their vast country.

I flew out to Adelaide and presented the first male and female study days there, but while I was at the airport gate ready to board my onward flight to Canberra, I had a distraught telephone call from Jo, my daughter-in-law. My only granddaughter, Maggie, aged just one year of age, had been diagnosed with leukaemia. I broke down and two air hostesses led me gently onto the plane.

I had to continue my month-long tour even though I wanted to fly home immediately. The Australian physiotherapists with whom I was billeted were wonderful. Email had just arrived and they emailed ahead to let each other know the ghastly news and to be ready with Australian red wine when I finished my day's lecturing.

The lecture in Melbourne was something different. I was given the title of 'Sex on Valentine's Day' and I think I gave them what they wanted. I ramped it up so it was a bit like *Sex and the City* (Miss Orme wasn't there). I talked about women doing their pelvic floor exercises to enhance their sex lives and gain multiple orgasms. I discussed anorgasmia, when women were unable to gain an orgasm, and the value of vibrators as part of sexual activity with or without a partner. Rabbit or dolphin, they could choose! I disclosed that I had one lady of ninety years of age who felt that the sensation of her orgasm was reduced, so I advised her (or her husband) to buy a vibrator, and the next time she came to see me she beamed like a Cheshire cat. Bless her! I mentioned that sex was not just for the young and body beautiful. Regrettably, I forgot to mention that the disabled had needs too. I mentioned the importance of foreplay for women who have vaginal dryness. I commented that during intercourse women needed to relax. 'Lie back and think of Australia,' I said, whereupon the audience shouted in unison, 'In Australia, we lie back and think of England!' How awesome! I mentioned that I thought that the female ejaculation was a myth. (If you look online at videos of women who swear that they ejaculate at orgasm, you can see urine spurting from their urethra.) Hats off to these clever women, who pass urinary leakage off to their partner as ejaculation! I regaled the audience with statistics about the time men take to achieve ejaculation (average five and a half minutes, longest forty minutes – but he went to sleep!). Naturally, I mentioned how I found that pelvic floor exercises helped to regain erectile function in some men. Use it or lose it! Years later, physios from Australia came up to me at international conferences, asked about my granddaughter's health and mentioned that they would never forget my Valentine's Day lecture! Oh dear...

The Antipodean tour consisted of a female continence day, then a male continence day in each city, followed by a day flying to the next destination. It was full on with no respite. The Australian physios dared me to pack the male plastic model in the top of my hand baggage so that the penis would spring up and startle the staff at customs. I conformed to their ribald suggestion, but luckily, I was never stopped and searched! I stayed with superb, dedicated physios in Adelaide, Canberra, Melbourne, Hobart, Brisbane, Christchurch, Newcastle and Sydney. In Tasmania, I stayed with Sylvia, a friend from our set at The London Hospital, and spent a few delightful days with her. She bought a new car for the occasion which she named 'Grace' and she proudly showed me around her beautiful island with its lush vegetation. Sadly, the ghastly forest fires in 2019 have devastated the trees and bushes in Tassie so that where Sylvia and I went on an exquisite tree-top walk, there is only a twisted iron walkway surrounded by charred branches and blackened stumps. Apparently, the unique alpine peat areas burned for months.

There was not much time for sightseeing in Australia, but visiting Blundell's Cottage in Canberra was unforgettable as I admired the wooden home and woodworking tools of some of my early ancestors. My maiden name was Blundell. It was Blundell himself who built the wooden bridge over the river nearby. I am proud to say that on my father's side, I come from a long line of carpenters, shop-front fitters and coffin-makers. My father had a love affair with wood and hated anything made of plastic. I guess inheriting a dollop of DNA from my forebears with their practical skills may well be linked to my choice of selecting an active physical profession.

I finished the month-long tour, rushed back to Maggie's cot in Bristol Children's Hospital and took my turn in staying with her both during the day and at night. After the cruel chemotherapy, lasting six months, mercifully Maggie was cured. Thanks to the expert care she had in Bristol, today she is a delightful, fit and healthy seventeen-year-old (with ten GCSEs) and has a lovely sister, Charlie (named after one of the nurses), aged sixteen years.

Out of the blue, I received a brown envelope marked 'On Her Majesty's Service', which looked like a tax demand. When I opened it, I was surprised and delighted to read that I was to be made a Member of the Order of the British Empire (MBE) in the New Year's Honours list. Proudly, I told three people, who were sworn to secrecy. My partner, Nick, was absolutely delighted for me, my son, Martin, said he was going to get a new suit (and shoes), and my daughter, Claire, was going shopping. I started a diet. Oh, and I developed an overly engrossing interest in hats!

That night, I awoke at 3am and wondered if I could curtsey without wobbling. I got up and performed the type of nude curtsey that would make your toes curl! But I didn't wobble. Well, bits of me might have.

I was informed that I could take three guests to the palace, so I invited Claire, Martin and my daughter-in-law, Jo. Nick kindly let Jo have his place as she had not been well and had experienced a tough time.

May 4th 2014 was a most memorable day. We stayed the night before with the family close to the palace at the Premier Inn at County Hall. In the morning I asked Nick if he could kindly go into the bathroom as I wanted to pop on my new Spanx. 'I'm going nowhere,' he retorted, and then poured me into this figure-hugging piece of kit (this is now for sale: used only once – by royal appointment). The killer heels have gone to a lucky charity shop.

Claire, Martin, Jo and myself hopped into a taxi, and Martin asked the driver to drive down the Mall. 'I know you,' the taxi driver replied. 'Aren't you the guy from *One Man and His Campervan*? My mother likes you.'

After a security search where a mirror was pushed under the taxi while our passports were inspected, we were dropped off under the impressive portico of Buckingham Palace and mounted the red-carpeted stairs, where I was directed to the right and my guests were directed to the ballroom on the left. As we were early, they sat graciously in the front row and appeared in everyone's photographs.

While the recipients waited in the throne room, we were instructed to walk up to one courtier and wait for our name to be called, then to walk to level with HRH Prince Charles turn, and walk three paces forwards, curtsey and shake his hand.

While I was waiting next in line, I had butterflies in my tummy, a fuzzy, fluttery feeling caused by the release of adrenaline reducing the blood flow to the stomach, which is a symptom of social anxiety disorder. This was a feeling that I had not experienced before or since. When I received my fellowship, I was emotional and shed a tear, but this was a truly wonderfully humbling honour.

I was announced, walked the walk and performed a curtsey (fully clothed) to HRH Prince Charles, who pinned my MBE onto a clip which was already in place and asked me, 'How long have you been a physiotherapist?'

I was ready for him, so answered, 'I have been a general physiotherapist for forty years but for the last ten years I have been treating men with pelvic floor exercises for erectile dysfunction.'

He grinned, then controlled himself, leaned forwards and whispered, 'Does it work?'

I replied, 'Yes, my research has shown that it is successful. I have been all round the world lecturing on the subject.'

'How did you get into this area?' he quizzed, to which I replied, 'I have been treating men's incontinence problems and have found that it helped with their erections.'

'Very good, very good,' he commented, as he smiled broadly and shook my hand again to signal the end of our conversation.

I took three wobble-free steps backwards (really difficult in sling-backs), turned and joined the back row of the guests.

My guests could not hear the comments but guessed from the laughter just what their mother was saying. When I arrived home, I sent HRH Prince Charles the book that I had written, which had a cartoon on every page titled '*Pump Up Your Penis*', and inscribed it 'To Prince Charles, for amusement only.' His head of household wrote back to say that HRH Prince Charles was indeed amused.

After the photo session at the palace, we walked to the gates and noticed my friend Kay with Maggie and Charlie peering through the railings. I was the proudest Gran Gran at the Palace. I hoped that they would remember this special day. Certainly, I would never forget. We returned to the hotel so that I could remove my Spanx. What a relief! Way better than an orgasm...

That evening, Nick took the family and those who had nominated me for my MBE to the Flyfishers' Club in London for what can only be termed a banquet, where I proudly wore my new badge of honour. I was beyond happy. Everyone ought to have their day and, thanks to some very generous people, I certainly had mine.

The next day we motored down the M4 to the Pear Tree at Purton where we had a celebratory lunch with twenty-five family members and twenty-five friends. I used this as an opportunity to thank the movers and shakers:

'A big thank you to Claire and Martin for kindly hosting my celebratory party, to Martin for his witty speech and to Claire for helping me to choose my outfit. I am so proud of both of you and I love you lots.

'It is splendid to be sharing this day with my wonderful family and special friends. Thank you to each one of you for being here with me on this happy occasion.

'Seeing Prince Charles was very emotional, moving and for the first time in my life I felt humble. It was like a dream, but it did happen because I have woken up this morning with a medal.

'I would like to express my gratitude to a very special lady – to Ros, my former physiotherapy manager at the Somerset Nuffield Hospital at Taunton. Over thirteen years ago, I left Chesham Bois in tears and came down to Devon for a new life. Ros welcomed me into the physiotherapy department, where I set up the continence clinic, and she allowed me to slip in my research patients with erectile dysfunction. Following my PhD, she kindly nominated me for a fellowship of The Chartered Society of Physiotherapy and then instigated my appointment as a consultant physiotherapist. Thank you, Ros. You are the best.

'Importantly today, I would like to show my sincere appreciation to three generous and warm-hearted colleagues to Claire Oldroyd, Kay Crotty and Mark Speakman for so kindly nominating me for my MBE. It is a wonderful honour which, as you know, means more than the world to me.

'I was party to an email that Nigel Watling sent to Mick Swinn on seeing my name in the New Year's Honours list, which read, "This is what a bit of bum-clenching can do!"

'So, gentlemen, do your pelvic floor exercises, for the boys it is never too early to start.

'After all, Nick has said that my MBE stands for "Making Better Erections".

'I would like to raise a toast to the real stars of today to: Ros, Claire, Kay and Mark, and to Nick, my lovely family and wonderful friends.'

I continued to work at the Somerset Nuffield Hospital as a consultant in the consulting rooms and loved the work there. It was a joy to be able to throw away my uniform and wear my own smart clothes (bought specially!). Unashamedly, I loved seeing the brass plate '**Professor Grace Dorey**' which was placed on my consulting room door. It was rather impressive to have a large desk to sit behind and certainly beat balancing a clipboard with the patient's notes wavering precariously on my knee! I treated men and women with all sorts of urinary and faecal incontinence and sex-related issues. Each patient would leave with a relevant self-help book. I had written eight by now in order to cover each condition. Whether it was the opulent consulting room suite or whether it was the rather grand desk, patients seemed to give me more respect in my new role. Perhaps it was the new swish outfits! I would be greeted with, 'Good morning, Professor Dorey,' or, 'Good morning, Prof,' as if they had never met a person with such a grand title. I admit it felt good. I gave each patient the benefit of my knowledge based on the latest research.

As a physiotherapy student, I never even dreamed that I would end my career as a consultant physiotherapist on a level with medical consultants. I knew that I was dedicated and always wanted to achieve, but this was more than I ever thought possible. When I trained, we were all generalists; there were no specialist areas, no extended scope practitioners and certainly no consultant posts.

Whurr Publishers kindly published my thesis as a textbook titled *Pelvic Floor Exercises for Erectile Dysfunction*, and I worked steadily and precisely to update my textbook which was published by Wiley with a new title – *Pelvic Dysfunction in Men* – which embraced the diagnosis and treatment of incontinence and erectile dysfunction in men. I receive a small amount of royalties from these books and an even smaller amount from the chapters that I have written for other authors' textbooks. I considered it was a great honour to be asked to write a chapter for my colleagues.

This was a very special time of my life. It was important to keep conversant with the cutting edge of the profession and meet physios from around the world at the international conferences. I was able to gain sponsorship to attend the International Continence Society conferences in places like Rotterdam, Monaco, Paris, Florence, Montreal, Barcelona and Christchurch, where I often submitted a presentation.

I proudly presented the results of my PhD research to delegates at the International Continence Society UK, where I followed a male registrar who showed a slide of a man with a bright yellow banana poking out from his trousers. I started my lecture by showing the anatomy of the penis and added, 'I would like to show the previous speaker what a penis looks like...' Because I presented a randomised controlled trial, I was fortunate to win the prize for the best presentation. I was unable to stop crying! Pretty pathetic, I know.

At one presentation, I noticed that when I stepped onto the podium, there was no monitor. I delivered my lecture by looking round and referring to the screen, which was rather awkward and a tad unprofessional. It was only when I left the stage, that I noticed that the monitor was placed on the floor behind the lectern and would be only visible to the taller speakers but was totally obscured by the pedestal to little lecturers like me. I should have brought a stool to stand on (or the dreaded massage platform!).

If the conference committee decided that the presentation was not suitable for the podium, they asked delegates to submit a poster. This was an absolute pain. It meant designing an eye-catching poster on the computer and having it made up by a print shop. I also had to purchase a poster-carrying tube and bring this unwieldly thing with me on the plane to the conference. What was worse was that you were expected to stay by your poster at set times, such as the coffee and tea breaks, and answer questions from interested (or not) delegates.

I used to go to conferences with my physio colleagues Jane and Kay, who would share the room of the physio who had been sponsored (usually me). We only attended the lectures that interested us so made enough time to see the top ten attractions in each city. We worked hard and played hard. Life was good.

During my career I wrote fifty-five academic papers in peer-reviewed journals; some papers were very similar but carefully directed to the readership. (Can you plagiarise your own work?) Also, I was asked to be a clinical reviewer for a number of journals, which was an honour that I took seriously.

I was invited to give lectures to students, physios, nurses, GPs, consultants and the general public. I really enjoyed preparing lectures with each audience in mind. Each lecture contained up-to-date research and several relevant cartoons to excite the delegates and amuse me too. (I had a cartoonist who was a friend of Martin's who kindly gave me 'Mum's rates'.)

One time, I lectured to a group of gynaecologists in Wales. I started by leaning over the low lectern and saying, 'Am I glad to have the opportunity to speak to you? Before you resort to surgery, make sure that your patients have seen a physiotherapist. My research has shown that in eighty per cent of cases we can resolve stress urinary incontinence with pelvic floor exercises. When you place surgical mesh round the urethra, it can lead to the mesh poking through the vaginal skin, pelvic pain and painful intercourse. The only patients that I refer for surgery are those who have severe prolapses.' Instead of being upset with me, I was approached by two gynaecologists to see if I would like to work in Wales.

One of the most important lectures of my career was to a group of leading urologists from around the world who met in Washington to discuss the best way to treat men with erectile dysfunction. I was flown out horizontally by Virgin business class and arrived fully prepared. Five minutes before I took the podium, I felt so ill that I thought I might have to be hospitalised. I had never felt so nervous. I recovered the moment I stood up to the lectern and gave my lecture on the conservative approach. From the post-lecture discussion, these urologists were extremely opinionated, arrogant and totally unwilling to take my research on board, believing that medication was the only way forward. 'Why not try both medication and pelvic floor exercises?' I added. You've probably guessed that the conference was funded by a drug company. The urologists all went out that evening for a jolly, while I took the opportunity to visit my charming nephew, Chris, and his family who lived in Arlington.

Very few companies sponsored pelvic floor physiotherapists, except those making continence pads, electrical stimulation machines and biofeedback apparatus. Suddenly out of the blue, I was asked to link in with Dr Andrew Siegel, a forward-thinking urologist from New Jersey, America, who had designed a small weight for men to lift on their erect penis. I was most impressed with this product called Private Gym, with its accompanying CD, but more than ever I was delighted that a urologist understood and embraced the physical approach. I was asked to write the foreword to his excellent textbook *Male Pelvic Fitness*. It is worth a read. The book, not the foreword – well, perhaps both.

In 2016, after fifty-four years as a physiotherapist, I decided to hang up my non-latex gloves. I resigned from the Somerset Nuffield Hospital and passed over the KY jelly to a younger continence physiotherapist.

When I retired, the Somerset Nuffield Hospital handed me the brass plate, '**Professor Grace Dorey**', which I keep proudly on my desk at home as a reminder of good times, and the University of the West of England generously awarded me the title of Emeritus Professor, a title which I can keep for life. So, gone are the days of being Miss Blundell, Mrs Dorey or even Dr Dorey; I can be Professor Grace Dorey for the rest of time. How cool is that?

Nick was exceptionally proud of my achievements. For years, he had visited me in Devon and I had flown over to Ireland to stay with him, so we had enjoyed a most exciting long-distant relationship. Once I had left Harley Street, North Devon District Hospital and The Somerset Nuffield Hospital, he asked me to live with him in Ireland. He vacated a wardrobe and I moved in (into the house, not the wardrobe). So begun another phase of my colourful life, this time one of affection, shared humour and pure contentment.

I agreed to present a final male continence study day at St Mary's Hospital in London in order to hand over to a couple of colleagues who were going to take this work on. The night before my valedictory lecture, I had acute pain in my heart at 4am and was rushed to the Hammersmith Hospital where they performed an angiogram and put a stent in my main coronary artery, which unfortunately blocked another coronary vessel and part of my cardiac septum. I was lying on my back on the table trying to be brave for a most uncomfortable two and a half hours, while my tears trickled into my ears.

That night I had a severe heart attack, where I vomited blood. It even poured out from my nose. The pain was unbearable, much worse than giving birth (without the joy of motherhood). While I was having this heart attack, the registrar stood over me and said that I would have to come back to the angiogram lab. I stuttered that I could not bear it and that if he wanted me to go back, I would need an anaesthetic. He said that only one in a hundred have anaesthesia, so I said, 'Then that will be me.' I did not see him again.

I was so upset to finish my career in this way and desperately hope that my work will continue to help both men and women in the future.

Nick flew over from Ireland to be with me; he packed for a few days and stayed for three months while I was admitted to the North Devon District Hospital in Barnstaple, then transferred to the Royal Devon and Exeter Hospital in Exeter where I underwent every cardiac test known to man (and a few unknown too!). In Exeter, the food was vastly improved from the dreary meals in Barnstaple and I found myself looking forward to Sunday lunch! The NHS should take a bow! There was only one other patient, Fran, patiently waiting for a pacemaker, who was stuck in the ward with me over Easter, a time when nothing medical happened, nothing, so we pretended that we were on holiday and greatly amused each other. It was wonderful to get visits from Richard and Ray, friends from the tennis club, who helped to lift my spirits, and my friend, Viv kindly visited, bringing a Scrabble board, which was so thoughtful and great fun, until she won!

After our 'holiday', I was given yet another angiogram (my fifth), this time through the artery in my right groin. Unfortunately, when I returned to the ward I bled profusely, felt dreadful, rung the bell and then collapsed. When I came to, a young trainee nurse was saying, 'Grace, Grace. Stay with us.' My blood pressure had plummeted to 65/30mmHg! A bit serious.

Nick was wonderfully supportive and caring; I was exceptionally lucky to have found such a kind and loving man. At last, I had the kind of relationship that, for years, I had craved.

In May 2017, I received a coronary bypass by Sir Malcolm Dalrymple-Hay in Derriford Hospital, Devon. I looked him up on the internet to see if he had been knighted for services to cardiology, but no, he was a baronet! I saw him privately to avoid waiting *at least* six months on the NHS. The NHS was failing many, many patients in need of an urgent bypass. I found it thoroughly inconceivable that ill patients were treated in this way. It seemed as if the NHS failed to care. I was delighted with my treatment. Going privately meant that I had jumped the queue and gave another patient my slot. It also meant that I could have the surgeon of my choice. Otherwise my treatment in the ward (would you believe I stayed in just three days?) was exactly the same as the NHS patients but infinitely more costly! When I was fit enough, I travelled back to Ireland with Nick. There, I attended cardiac rehabilitation classes for three months which were free as part of an Irish government initiative.

At eighty years of age, I continue to disgrace myself on the tennis courts (if wet, and it often is, we play table tennis), I have started the amazing sport of pickleball indoors and have taken up Silver Swans ballet for ladies fifty-five years and over – possibly the biggest joke in my life! Don't ask. I am the worst in the class. I can't jump!

I live happily in Ireland with my 'lunchtime' patient, Nick, thirty-four years after I first met him. I would like to report that I have not missed my lunch since that life-changing day! We have a wonderful relationship. The ultimate.

I am blessed with a superb family, all of whom are taller than me, which they tell me is not difficult.

I would like to thank Miss Orme for giving her little student a chance to enter a fulfilling, rewarding and, at times, amusing profession.

It has been a privilege.

Afterword

Today's students can study for three years for a Batchelor of Science BSc (Hons) in physiotherapy at a recognised university, or in some locations they can serve an apprenticeship. They need three relevant A-levels and a desire to help people regain normal physical function, movement and independence. Unlike the days in the 1950s, when physiotherapists were taught massage, electrotherapy and exercises, the syllabus has expanded exponentially and is more research-based. We treated patients in a certain way because we were told it would help. Now only treatment that has been shown to be effective through evidence-based research is taught to students. Importantly, students are taught to be analytical when critically reviewing scientific papers.

During training, students go on clinical placements to various hospitals or clinics where they are mentored and assessed by senior physiotherapists. There are so many specialist areas that it is impossible to cover all of them during training, so after qualification, students are encouraged to work at a large NHS hospital where for two years they can do rotations to a number of different disciplines such as: outpatients, orthopaedics, neurology, paediatrics, respiratory and geriatrics. Students are encouraged to keep a CSP ePortfolio and learning hub document, so that they can be assessed as they learn new skills. Continuing Professional Development is *expected* from today's physiotherapists. The range of skills needed are different for each speciality, and an ambitious physiotherapist can diversify into a specialist area, read for a MSc and PhD, and become a consultant physiotherapist. Physiotherapists may prefer to be generalists in private practice or specialise in one area such as shoulders or hand therapy. Some may prefer to take on a managerial role.

Physiotherapy covers many diverse areas, and physiotherapists tend to specialise in one particular area. It would be impossible to have an in-depth knowledge of all the specialist areas, which indicates just how much the profession has grown. There are thirty professional networks recognised by the CSP, some of which focus on specific patient populations such as children, people with learning difficulties or older people. Some focus on the type of medical speciality such as neurology; intensive care; pelvic, obstetric, and gynaecological; or oncology and palliative care. Others focus on specific techniques such as acupuncture and aquatic therapy. There is even a network for those performing animal therapy. How lovely is that.

Physiotherapy is not a well-paid profession in the UK. Physiotherapists start out with a salary of £21,176, which can be enhanced with a London weighting. Salaries increase as physiotherapists become more experienced and gain senior posts and managerial roles. I found that private practice and lecturing were better-paid options. Also, when I helped to design the male pelvic floor model, it was better to have a percentage of the cost of models sold, rather than receive a flat fee!

Physiotherapists will never be top earners like bankers, the legal profession and those in industry, but they will have an interesting and active role where they help people to develop their full physical potential and have the satisfaction of a job well done. Every day is different, every patient reacts in a different way to a similar medical problem and it is fascinating to be able to modify your approach to gain the patient's trust and responsiveness, so that between the two of you, their condition can improve and hopefully be cured. Physiotherapists and the other caring professions have an image which is rated very highly by the public. There are 58,000 members of The Chartered Society of Physiotherapy who can call themselves chartered physiotherapists. The title 'Physiotherapy' and 'Physiotherapist' is protected by those physiotherapists who become a member of the Health and Care Professions Council (HCPC), so only those who are qualified can call themselves a physiotherapist. I am proud to have spent my working life in this unique profession.

Since retirement, frequently I have been asked if I miss work. I do NOT miss getting up early five or six days a week, driving from Chesham Bois to Bushey in the rain, sleet or, sometimes, snow. In winter, I particularly hated travelling both ways in the dark. I dreaded the ice. Since retirement, I love the freedom of not having to get up early and go to work. The freedom of being able to play tennis with the seniors. I like the contented feeling of having done my bit and given what I believe to be my best for fifty-five years. I miss the salary! I miss the contact with my patients, the stimulation of diagnosing their problem and the joy of sharing their happiness when they are cured. I miss the warmth of my colleagues and their quick wit. Also, I miss the excitement of compiling my lectures and delivering them to (I hope) interested delegates. I miss the excitement of jumping on a plane and visiting other countries and meeting the delightful, dedicated physios from around the world. It may sound unbelievable, but most of all, I miss making my audiences smile!

Guidelines for Physiotherapists

Treat patients with respect and dignity.

Use treatments that have been proven by research.

Have an awesome sense of humour.

Guidelines for Patients

Remember physiotherapists have feelings.

Choose a qualified chartered physiotherapist – not an over-zealous ninety-year-old!

Amuse your physiotherapist.

Don't malinger (your physiotherapist will know).

On no account, sue!

Glossary

Alternating current Electric current that reverses its direction many times a second at regular intervals.

Amputee Person with limb removed by trauma or surgery.

Anal examination Testing the strength of the anal sphincter and pelvic floor muscles.

Anatomy Learning about the structure of the body.

Biofeedback machine Indicates the strength of the muscles.

Cadaver Dead body.

Calcaneal bone Heel bone.

Carpal tunnel syndrome Compression of the median nerve as it travels through the wrist.

Cervical spine Bones of the neck.

Clapping Percussion massage using cupped hands.

Club feet Congenital malformation of the feet.

Continence Ability to prevent leakage of urine.

Continuing Professional Development Record of what you experience, learn and apply.

Coronary bypass Surgery to restore normal blood flow to an obstructed coronary artery.

Cupping Using cupped hands to massage.

Cybex Trade name for machine which gives an opposite force to muscle work.

Cyriax manipulations Manipulations to click the joint, named after Dr James Cyriax.

Deep vein thrombosis Blockage of the deep vein in the calf by a blood clot.

Direct current Electric current flowing in one direction.

Dissection Cutting of a deceased body.

Effleurage Circular massage.

Electrical stimulation Electric impulses to gain a muscle contraction.

Erectile dysfunction Inability to gain an erection.

Extension Stretching a joint outwards.

Extra pyramidal system Part of the brain causing involuntary actions.

Femur Thigh bone.

Ferrule Rubber tip to prevent walking stick from slipping.

Flexion Bending a joint inwards.

Infrared irradiation Heat delivered by a luminous or non-luminous lamp.

Joint replacement Artificial joint replacing a natural joint.

Faecal incontinence Leakage of poo.

Faradism Rapidly alternating electric current to stimulate nerve and muscle activity.

Fibula Smaller bone in the lower leg.

Formalin Formaldehyde, a naturally occurring organic compound.

Hacking Light, fast movements performed with the side of the hands.

Harelip Congenital malformation of the upper lip.

Hydrotherapy Use of warm water to aid or resist movement.

Hysterical palsy Psychological distress affecting movement of a limb.

Interferential machine Two medium frequency currents cross and control pain.

Kneading Compression of skin and muscle by massage.

Kromayer Hand-held ultraviolet lamp.

Leukaemia Cancer starting in the bone marrow producing abnormal white cells.

Ligament Fibrous tissue holding a joint together.

Lumbar spine Bones of the lower back.

Lymph Clear fluid containing white blood cells

Maitland's mobilisations Passive movements of the vertebral spine (Grades 1-4).

Maitland's manipulations High velocity movements of the vertebral spine (Grade 5).

Massage Stroking and moving the soft tissues of the body.

Medicine ball Heavy exercise ball (1–5kg).

Multiple sclerosis Hard patches in brain and spinal cord affecting muscles and nerves.

Non-parametric tests Statistical tests not based on normal distribution of data.

Obturator nerve Nerve in the groin.

Osteoarthritis Breakdown of joint cartilage and bone, producing pain and stiffness.

Osteopathy Physical manipulation of muscle and bones.

Ovarian cancer Cancer of the ovaries.

Quadriceps femoris muscle Muscle on front of the thigh.

Parallel bars Two bars at hand height to aid walking.

Parametric tests Statistical tests based on normal distribution of data.

Petrissage Deep tissue massage.

Phallus Penis.

Phantom pain Pain that feels as if it is coming from an absent body part.

Physiology Study of the functions of the body.

Pituitary gland Master gland controlling other glands.

Plasma proteins Present in blood plasma transporting vitamins and hormones.

Police disclosure Identity and criminal record check for those working with people.

Post-prostatectomy incontinence Leakage of urine following prostate surgery.

Postural drainage Tilting of the body to drain the lungs of secretions.

Prolapse Sagging of the vaginal wall.

Proprioceptive Neuromuscular Facilitation (PNF) Advanced method of stretching and contracting muscles to improve muscular strength.

Prosthetic Artificial arm or leg.

Psittacosis Bacterial infection of parrots.

Psoriasis Red flaky scaly patches of skin.

Red blood corpuscles Transport oxygen and remove carbon dioxide from the body.

Renotin gel ionisation Direct current pushes gel into tissues as counter-irritant.

Rolling Massage technique where muscle is rolled.

Schnee four-cell bath Direct current used for treating painful ankles and feet.

Sciatica Pain down the back of the leg caused by pressure on the sciatic nerve.

Shortwave diathermy High-frequency energy as form of deep heat for painful joints.

Sinusoidal current Alternating current.

Slings Attached to a pulley to aid movement of a joint.

Stress urinary incontinence Leakage of urine during coughing, sneezing or exertion.

Suppurated Oozed pus.

Synovial sheath Protective sheath round a muscle tendon to provide smooth movement.

Tibia Large lower leg bone.

Thoracic spine Vertebra of the upper back.

Thyroid Gland producing thyroxine which regulates the body's energy.

Traction Stretching of the spine to relieve the pressure on the spinal nerves.

Transvestite A person who enjoys dressing as someone from the opposite sex.

Treadmill Moving and tilting floor used for walking and running.

Ultrasound Soundwaves higher than are audible that enhance healing.

Ultraviolet light Shorter wavelengths than visible light which tans the skin.

Urge urinary incontinence Leakage of urine preceded by a strong urge to pee.

Urinary incontinence Leakage of urine.

Vaginal examination Digital examination to test strength of the pelvic floor muscles.

Venous return of the blood Blood returning to the heart via the veins.

Vibrator Vibrating plastic phallus to produce an orgasm.

Wax treatment Warm molten paraffin wax to soothe painful hand and foot joints.

Wobbleboard Unstable board to stand on and develop core strength.

Acknowledgements

I would like to thank my son, Martin, and his partner, (Dr) Liz, for helping me to develop a 'readable book'. 'It has to have more of you in it,' they said in unison, so in response I have added details of my personal life, which I have kept locked away for years.

To Nick, who put up with my night-time terrors with fortitude as I wrote about my past life. Thank you for being there for me.

I am forever grateful for the support and humour of my friends. You know who you are, and you know how we have laughed and will continue to laugh.

My sincere gratitude goes to Miss Orme for accepting me to train as a physiotherapist. I hope that I haven't let you down.

I am indebted to my colleagues for making my working life so much fun.

To my many grateful patients, it has been a privilege to get to know you and be able to help you in some way.

The Author

Professor Grace Dorey MBE FCSP PhD has worked as a chartered physiotherapist for fifty-four years. She trained at The London Hospital, and has worked at the Harrow Physical Treatment Centre, Harrow Hospital, West Herts Hospital, Joseph Brant Memorial Hospital, Canada, Kodak Ltd and BUPA Hospital Bushey, where she was the physiotherapy manager for seventeen years. She also ran a private practice in Chesham Bois and Harley Street. She set up a continence clinic at The Somerset Nuffield Hospital and at North Devon District Hospital, Barnstaple. Following the stunning result of her PhD research titled 'Pelvic Floor Exercises for Erectile Dysfunction', Grace has lectured internationally. She is the author of three textbooks and eight self-help books.

She has a daughter, a son and two granddaughters, and lives in Ireland with her partner, Nick.

Other Books
by the Same Author

Barking Mad in Barnstaple The diary of an elderly professor of physiotherapy who was given a fluffy Golden Retriever puppy by her partner for Christmas and who adamantly believed that puppy training was easy and would produce the perfect dog. William remained uncontrolled, despite diligently attending all the dog training classes available in Devon and the surrounding counties.

William: Still Barking continues to monitor the 'hound from hell' and recalls how the local farmer threatened to shoot him, how he exterminated rabbits, birds and mice, how the grandchildren were frightened of him, and how the family were concerned that an uncontrolled dog, the size of a rogue elephant, would be too strong for his owner.

A Puppy the Size of a Pony is a sequel to *Barking Mad in Barnstaple* and *William: Still Barking*, and completes the trilogy by Grace Dorey, which continues to monitor this rogue Retriever, while he grapples with his determination to escape, hones his hunting skills by chasing foxes, pheasants and deer, and displays a passionate love affair with anything muddy. Despite all his numerous imperfections, and there are many, he forms a special bond with his owner, so that she finds it a privilege to love and own a zany, hair-brained comedian called 'William'.

Don't Expect the Vet to Laugh This lively and amusing book follows the path of two gorgeous black flat coat Retrievers from puppyhood to something resembling adulthood, and includes their many foibles and wayward characteristics. It includes their friendship with William, the star of three previous books, until mayhem rules and threatens to exasperate their normally cheerful owner.

Clench It or Drench It! Self-help book for women with urinary leakage.

Love Your Gusset: Making Friends with Your Pelvic Floor Cartoon book for women with incontinence, sexual dysfunction and an outrageous sense of humour.

Make It or Fake It! Self-help book for women with sexual dysfunction.

Prevent It! Guide for men and women with leakage from the back passage.

Use It or Lose It! Self-help book for men with urinary leakage and erectile dysfunction.

Living and Loving After Prostate Surgery Self-help book for men with incontinence and erectile dysfunction after prostate surgery.

Stronger and Longer! Guide on improving erections with pelvic floor exercises.

Pump Up Your Penis: Easy Exercises to Strengthen Your Erection Cartoon book for men with erectile dysfunction and a wild sense of humour.

Pelvic Dysfunction in Men: Diagnosis and Treatment of Male Incontinence and Erectile Dysfunction Textbook.

Pelvic Floor Exercises for Erectile Dysfunction Textbook.